BELIEVING

BELIEVING

Sermons by Horton Davies

EDITED BY
JOHN BOOTY AND
MARIE-HÉLÈNE DAVIES

Eugene, Oregon

BELIEVING
Sermons by Horton Davies

Copyright © 2007 Marie-Hélène Davies. All rights reserved. Except for brief quotations in critical publications or reviews, no part of this book may be reproduced in any manner without prior written permission from the publisher. Write: Permissions, Wipf & Stock, 199 W. 8th Ave., Eugene, OR 97401.

ISBN 10: 1-55635-071-6
ISBN 13: 978-1-55635-071-9

Manufactured in the U.S.A.

CONTENTS

Foreword / vii
Acknowledgments / ix
Introduction / xi

I Believe

Lord, I Believe, Help My Unbelief / 3
A Victorious Faith: Conquering Skepticism / 9

I Believe in God the Father Almighty

The Hidden God / 17
The God of Nature and the God of Grace / 21
The Severity of God / 25
All Things Work Together / 29

I Believe in Jesus His Only Son Our Lord

The Incarnation 1 / 35
The Incarnation 2 / 39
The Divinity of Our Lord 1 / 43
The Divinity of Our Lord 2 / 49
The Divinity of Our Lord 3 / 53
God's Covenant with Men / 57
The Atonement: Divine Blood-Transfusion / 63
The Meaning of the Cross 1 / 67
The Meaning of the Cross 2 / 71
The Verdict on the Cross / 75
The Meaning of the Resurrection Today / 79

I Believe in the Holy Spirit

The Holy Spirit / 87
The Harvest of the Holy Spirit / 91

I Believe in the Holy Catholic Church

Why I Believe in the Holy Catholic Church / 97
A Victorious Faith: Conquering Racial Tension / 103
Wanted: Our Own Pentecost as a Company of the Church of Christ / 107
Wanted: A Perpetual Pentecost / 111
Christianity as the Servant Church / 115

I Believe in the Communion of Saints

All Saints' Day / 121
The Living Union of Christ and His Disciples / 125
Saints Alive / 131

I Believe in the Forgiveness of Sins

Sin Is Rebellion Against God / 137

I Believe in Life Eternal

Immortality / 145
Eternal Life: Here & Hereafter / 149
Terminus Becomes Tunnel / 151

The Fruit of Belief: Joy

Essentials of Happiness / 159

FOREWORD

What a very rich career Horton Davies had! Born in Wales of devout parents in 1916, he graduated from Edinburgh University, served in London during the Blitz, worked for several years in South Africa during the dark days of apartheid, and then moved to a teaching post at Princeton University. That is the skeleton of a remarkable ministry which enabled him to produce 35 learned books on a variety of issues. Although I never had the privilege of meeting him, his death in 2004 came as a sadness to me, because his writings were so well known that it was as if I had lost a good friend.

What I especially valued in Professor Davies was the seamlessness of his faith and academic work. Such was his commitment to the Christian faith, that it was never for him a dull and boring subject for intellectual enquiry. His faith was real and he tackled every topic and task with passionate interest.

Passion, indeed, runs like a golden thread through this collection of addresses. As I read the sermons in draft form I found myself reflecting on the difference between a great deal of modern preaching and the focus and themes of Horton's addresses. Listening these days, in retirement, to the preaching of others I confess with dismay that so many sermons lack theological and intellectual depth, so many preachers lack passion and—this is the most worrying part—so many addresses seem to spring from hasty preparation, lacking in reflection.

None of that will be found in this anthology. Here we find addresses that are well prepared and aimed at intelligent people. Horton acknowledges the doubts and difficulties of modern people and he seeks to speak to his fellow men and women in terms and in a language that they will understand. He drew upon a well-stocked mind and, from a vast knowledge of literature and the experience of life, was able to inform and entertain his listeners. Perhaps it was the influence of his skill as a teacher that led to such a fierce commitment to connecting with others. Whether this is so or not, it is impossible to read any one of his addresses without knowing what his intention was in preaching it. With rigor he attempted to draw his listeners to a decision.

Indeed, this stress on communication made his preaching 'evangelical' in the best way that noble word is understood. Not for him fundamentalism, because his love of learning and commitment to truth, did not allow him to submit to superficial conclusions. However, neither was he a vague liberal to whom all forms of knowledge are provisional. He believed, and believed passionately; and such believing in the truth of the Christian faith was nourished by scholarship and by a life-long faith in his Lord. He called people to personal commitment.

Is such preaching dated these days? Preaching that is relevant has to be localised and contemporary. From that perspective Horton's preaching has to be read in the light of his time, just as we have to read Augustine's sermons in the same way. But that does not mean that great sermons are dated, if, by that, we mean that they are no longer meaningful for our time. Horton's addresses have much to contribute to our thinking today. I am convinced that our contemporaries will respond positively to carefully crafted addresses, honed by deep knowledge of the faith and reason.

Horton Davies, who died in 2004 at the great age of 88, stands in a great tradition of eminent Welsh preachers who have graced the pulpit. This anthology is a not only a tribute to a great teacher but also a vivid example of a great one at work.

George Carey
Lord Carey of Clifton
103rd Archbishop of Canterbury, 1991–2002

ACKNOWLEDGMENTS

I WANT to thank Ted Lewis, from Wipf and Stock Publishers for agreeing readily to publish theological and doctrinal sermons from my late husband. I also want to express my gratitude to John Booty, the first graduate student of my husband in Princeton, who guided me as to the choice and order of the present sermons, wrote the major part of the introduction and is ready to assist me for another volume. He and his wife greeted me to their home and have been a moral as well as an intellectual support. And I thank Princeton University, without whose technology I would still be typing the sermon corpus as well as the Princeton Religion Department whose door has always been open and whose warmth has provided a steady support.

To all, Horton would have been grateful, yet not surprised for he knew their boundless compassion.

INTRODUCTION

Background

HORTON DAVIES was Putnam Professor of Religion at Princeton University where his teaching was focused on the history and liturgics of Christianity. It was in relation to his interest in and knowledge of the Western church that he considered the art of preaching. Beginning with his Oxford University doctoral dissertation, "The Worship of the English Puritans," published in 1948, Davies demonstrated his acute understanding of the Free Church tradition of Christian worship in England, especially at its beginnings in the 16th and 17th centuries. Chapter 12 considers Puritan preaching as central to the tradition. He wrote:

> The importance of preaching consisted in the fact that it was the declaration by the preacher of the revelation of God, confirmed in the hearts of the believers by the interior testimony of the Holy Spirit. (Page 182)

This declaration was rooted in a theological base which included the awareness of "the great abyss that separated God from man." It was of infinite importance that "God should cross that abyss and speak to the Christian through the sermon," rather than that the Christian "should traverse it in prayer or praise" (Page 183).

For the 16th century Reform Theologians, such as Peter Martyr Vermigli, the sacraments were the "invisible words of God," serving in dramatic form, as it were, but for many the preaching of the Word of God was preeminent, not in place of the sacraments but as with ingredients of the sacraments of Baptism and the Lord's Supper.

Nevertheless the Puritan emphasis was on the sermon and the preacher. Davies wrote: "The preacher was the man of God, the prophet, who declared to the congregation the 'mystery' of the Gospel, unfolding the whole plan of salvation, under compulsion to bring men to the parting of the ways that lead to salvation or damnation" (Page 185). For the Puritan "the exposition and discussion of the Scripture" was "the outstanding feature of their worship" (Page 190).

Beyond and beneath Davies's study of Puritan worship is the Free Church tradition, with its influence on his understanding of preaching, was the example of his father, the Reverend David Dorian Marlais Davies, who for more than fifty years served congregations of the Congregational Church "in Wales, England, Scotland and the Channel Islands." In his book *Varieties of English Preaching: 1900–1960* (1963), Davies remembers his father fondly and with great respect for the man and for the dedicated and talented preacher. With such a father "how could one doubt that the ministry was a high calling and preaching a pre-eminent calling?" (Pages 13 & 14). He witnessed a wide range of people, from Welsh miners to doctors, professors, and naval officers arrive at church worried and hearing David Davies preach the word "leave with a clearer conviction and the courage of faith" (Page 14).

In *Varieties of English Preaching* Horton Davies discusses the task of the preacher. First is apologetical preaching, vindicating the Christian faith, refuting barriers to that faith and "demonstrating that the Gospel of God as transforming truth fulfills "the nature and destiny of man." Examples of such preaching are to be found in the sermons of Archbishop Temple and Professor Herbert Farmer (Page 29). The second task is "to deepen the congregation's understanding of God and, assisted by the interior power of the Holy Spirit in preacher and congregation alike, to awaken and confirm faith" (Page 30). Thus there is a teaching function and the task of arousing faith in the worshipers hearing the preacher. As the sermons in this volume affirm, Davies was both a preacher and a prophet, challenging his auditors to believe and to act in accordance with belief. This is "the expository type of preaching" exemplified in the sermons of Dr. W. Sangster, in England, Dr. James Stewart of the Church of Scotland, and the Rev. John R. W. Stott of the Church of England" (Page 30–31). The third task of the preacher, related to the second, "is to teach the holy love of God so as to elicit the response of adoration" (Page 31). Examples of such preaching are to be found in the sermons of Dr. J. H. Jowett and Dean Inge, proponents of Christ in mysticism. Davies also points to the Roman Catholic tradition as a whole in which devotional preaching flowers "in the rich loam of the Roman liturgy." Davies came to possess a wide and rich knowledge of liturgy in the various denominational expressions and viewed his own preaching not in isolation from but in the context of liturgical worship as a whole. The fourth task is to assist the members of the congregation "to rediscover that their near or remote neighbors of every race and class are brothers in Christ. The motivation is compassion

Introduction

(literally a suffering with others), not sentimentality" (Page 32). Such moral or ethical preaching, exemplified by Henley Henson and William Temple, with their quest for social justice, was inspired in part by Davies's experience preaching in London during the horrors of World War II, in South Africa during the apartheid regime, and in the United States during the Civil Rights movement of the 1950s and 60s.

Davies's sermons in this volume exhibit the realization of these four tasks. Under the title of apologetic preaching there are many examples. I think of his sermon on "The Hidden God" exposing Isaiah 45:15. Here, during World War II, he remembers the pain and agony, the 10 million deaths of World War I, the Great War, and asks "Where was God then? Where is God today?" and seeks to answer the question in terms of God's "dwelling in light unapproachable," God's transcendence, but also in relation to the profound insight into God's respect for humanity. "He will not thrust himself upon men. If He did, He would undo His own works in us: He would take from us the most precious thing we have—our freedom of choice and will." But, God, though hidden, is not absent. The Incarnation speaks to how God came hidden in the form of Christ, for us and for our salvation.

In sermons on the Incarnation Davies exhibits the challenge of the second task, teaching faith to arouse an awakening faith. He speaks in plain terms, teaching that at Christmas time "we celebrate not the rising of man to deity: but the infinite condescension of God to mankind. The Virgin Birth is simply a poetical and pictorial way of suggesting that the birth of Jesus was no ordinary birth. It was the spirit of divine intervention, with human cooperation, of the spirit of God and of Mary." And so he proceeds ending with the assertion that the last word is not "argument: it is adoration in the presence of Christ." To adore is to feel faith awakening, belief affirmed as we fall down before the One who is God incarnate. Here is evidence to the third task: to respond is properly adoration resulting in the life of the devout mystic or the ordinary way of life transformed by the Holy Spirit working in us.

Davies's involvement in the fourth task was focused on realizing the effects of faith in life individually and corporately. His sermon called "A Victorious Faith: Conquering Racial Tension" given at the Congregational Church of Brookfield, Connecticut, on July 15, 1959, was clearly exemplary of the fourth task. Beginning with St. Paul (Galatians 3:26–28), Davies set forth the two great classes of the church's inter-racial Charter that we are all God's adopted children and that "Christ's new family, the new 'Christian race' has overcome racial prejudice, class prejudice, educational prejudice and sexual prejudice." It is not surprising that the world seeks to destroy such revolutionary affirmations. The preacher was clearly inspired by the Holy

Introduction

Spirit, stating with various illustrations that to be a disciple of Christ is to affirm the infinite worth of all people, to fight for justice for all.

This does not mean that Davies ultimately focused on social justice. Such justice was the fruit of faith in God, in Christ, by means of the Holy Spirit. A vital faith was integrally relational. First, it was so in relation to the church. Davies could be severely critical of the church when it mirrored the faulty society around it rather than reflecting the Kingdom of God. But, he affirmed that it was still, under God, the Holy, Catholic and Apostolic church. Believing is mainly belonging to a community that affirms the Lordship of Jesus Christ. And this affirmation leads to relationships to the world, the society to which it is sent by Christ with the message of love, reconciliation, forgiveness, peace and justice. Davies quotes Dietrich Bonhoeffer as writing: "The Church is her true self only when she exists for humanity." Davies adds:

> In the past the church has been an institution alongside, not the leaven within the world it is meant to change . . . Christ is the man for others; the church is men and women for others. This is the suggestion of the central Christian affirmation of the Incarnation where we see the Supreme as servant.

Christian joy according to Davies involves "a good conscience": freedom "from resentment against others or against life," the affirmation of faith, the realization of trust, and finally "the deepest source of joy is a selfless spirit that forgets itself and its worries in seeking the good of others." He recalls a newspaper photograph taken during the fire raids on London during the second World War, showing two elderly nuns in the midst of the smoke and terror delivering "trays of tea to the exhausted fire-fighters, unaware of their own danger, heroic, undisturbed." He concludes, "They had all four secrets of Christian joy."

In so speaking, Davies was bidding his listeners "to follow Christ, thus receiving that which the ever-living Christ promises you in his service, a clear conscience, the removal of bitterness, the faith and love that cast out fear and the selflessness of the Cross."

Admittedly, reading the sermons of Horton Davies is not the same as hearing him preach them. But reading the few sermons that follow in this book gives you, and all of us, an opportunity to benefit from his inspiration, as in all good preaching, as spirit speaks to spirit, inspired by the Holy Spirit of God.

Introduction

Artistry

Although most of the sermons in this collection were often youth sermons, yet one can find in them the artistry that led Horton to write later about the Puritan sermons and about the "metaphysical preachers." Indeed Davies took sermons very seriously as the exposition of the Word of God. His family would know that on the morning of his preaching they had to make themselves scarce, so high was the level of intensity of the preacher. When in the pulpit, the sermons were delivered with controlled Welsh passion, the voice strong and persuasive, trying to keep his voice from falling at the end of sentences. This was a completely different manner from the humble and gentle delivery of his lectures or precepts. He preached with great conviction, very much aware of the responsibility that preaching entailed, on truth, the human condition and the turmoils of the world he lived in.

Typically a sermon would be 4 to 6 single-spaced typewritten pages in length and very compact. Davies preferred the plain style of the Puritans, designed to move his flock to repentance and transform them into soldiers of Christ or saints. However, if judgment was passed, Davies rarely resorted to invective. In "Eternal Life: Heaven and Hell" he said:

> That kind of preaching has gone. It has gone because it is not the purpose of our Faith to offer men salvation as a fire-escape. It has gone because its conception of God and of our Lord was vindictive, cruel and unworthy. But, and here lies the mistake, we have rejected the Christian doctrine of judgment because the imagery in which it was clothed was liable to be crudely used.

As an ecumenist, he alternatively followed the Christian calendar without necessarily adhering to the lectionary, or took up the Creed and atypically for modern Puritans, did not pursue the expository of one of the books of the Bible. He adhered faithfully to Christological themes, in exegesis and applications of Scripture related to contemporary situations. As in other sermons, we find that he is not heavy on Patristic learning or on citations from the Greek, Latin and Hebrew, or even on wit, since he was speaking to a regular congregation, mostly during a period of duress, the Second World War, the time of Apartheid in Africa, the time of racial unrest in America. The tone in general was honest and earnest; he used empathy and imagination and the application was understandable for all.

Introduction

The Use of History

History appears in many sermons under various forms.

For church history Davies has sympathy for doubting Thomas. He refers to Martin Luther, William Temple and William Carey, Barth and Gibson Winter, but also to St. Francis of Assisi and St. François Xavier. In a conversion story, he expresses admiration for Count Zizendorf, the founder of the Moravians. His modern saints are mainly Albert Schweitzer, Father Damien and an unnamed priest who spent the whole of Holy Week in jail, preaching to the inmates. He makes interesting rapprochements as between Aeschylus and Niebuhr in "A victorious faith conquering racial tension," as they both believe that it is in suffering that we learn.

Quotes

Davies also likes to quote from the learned. Many of the sermons start with a quote from Scripture, and sometimes the sermon itself is strewn with repetition of the initial scriptural text, as in "Essentials of Happiness." More often, he cites some of the expositors of Scripture. He often refers to Victor Murray and quotes him in "The Holy Spirit" and to Canon Cockin in "The harvest of the Holy Spirit" and John Wesley in "The Atonement" and "Authentic nonconformity." Expositors do not mean for him only church historians. He practices the belief in the priesthood of all believers by quoting writers and poets: in the "Atonement" he cites William James and G.K. Chesterton (also in "Terminus becomes tunnel"), in the "Incarnation" the poet Charles Lamb. In the same breath, in "God's covenant with men," Davies cites John Calvin and Hugh Lyon on the importance of belonging to a church to be a Christian. At the time of war, in "Christianity as the Servant Church" he expresses his admiration for the German Bonhoeffer's views on the true spirit of the church and both for him and Niemoller for their resistance to the Nazis. Sensitive to those of his church who come to church with honest doubt in "Lord, I believe, help my unbelief," he hopes that The Rev. Leslie Tizard's meditations on the subject will be useful. And yet he does not condone those who might use doubting as an excuse. He lashes them with the irony of Dr. J.S. Whale who satirizes those Christians who tend to take pictures of Christ instead of kneeling in front of him and serving. Using Dr. James Stewart in "Wanted a permanent Pentecost," and Katherine Mansfield in "Victorious faith conquering Skepticism," he scoffs at the perpetual seeker.

For hymns, his favorite authors are Charles Wesley: "For all the saints..." ("Saints Alive") ("The Hidden God") ("The Verdict"), Isaac Watts ("Why I

Introduction

Believe in the Holy Catholic Church") and Baxter's "Christ leads me through no darker rooms" ("Lord I Believe, Help My Unbelief").

Hymns appealed to the sensitivity he had developed as English major in Edinburgh, before taking his theological degree. So it is not surprising to find many references to literary figures from different backgrounds and convictions, in the craftsmanship of the sermons. Ahead comes Shakespeare, which Davies knew by rote since he had in his young days learnt the whole of the bard by heart and won the Shakespeare prize. He quotes Shylock's speech in *The Merchant of Venice* to awaken the conscience of those who might have some Nazi sympathy, Lady Macbeth's sleep-walking scene to show the need of a good conscience ("Essentials of happiness"), Henry Vth rallying his troops as an example of the need for courage ("The Living Union of Christ and his disciples"), Prospero's last will and testament at the end of *The Tempest* ("The Meaning of the Resurrection") and the *Sonnets* to show that there is only a matter of degree between human and divine love ("The Harvest of the Holy Spirit").

G.K. Chesterton and Dorothy Sayers and Katherine Mansfield have already been mentioned. He also uses modern novelists and dramatists. For instance in "Victorious faith conquering Skepticism" he summarizes the plot of Harold Frederic's *The damnation of Theron Ware, or Illumination* as an example of shallow skepticism and contrasts it with Mrs. Humphry Ward's *Robert Elsmere* as an example of earnest skepticism. In "The Severity of God" he summarizes Sutton Vane's play, *Outward bound*, made into a film called *Between two worlds* as an example of the divine Assize and the concept of judgment and retribution. In "The Verdict on the Cross" comes this quote from John Masefield *The trial of Jesus*: to the question of where is Christ now is answered: "Let loose in the world, lady, where neither Jew nor Roman can stop his truth." He also refers to the poets Hamilton King, Charles Lamb and David Thoreau, the American lover of Nature.

Historical References

Historical references are used in various contexts. For explanation of the Covenant, for instance, he refers to an exhibition of medieval charters between the King of England and his subjects, on sight at the Bodleian Library. As an indirect encouragement to resistance under tyranny in a mixed congregation which might have contained Nazi-sympathizers, he refers to the Spartans or to the early Christians in the catacombs of Rome. There are many examples.

Introduction

Davies is therefore aware of the particular strain imposed by the modern world on the faith of his congregation. There are three main historical situations he addresses.

The first is World War II. The allusions are frequent: to the Battle of Britain in "Terminus becomes tunnel," to Ann Franck in "Victorious faith conquering Skepticism." He does not launder the atrocities of the day. In "All things work together for those who love God," he says:

> Sodom and Gomorrah, Nineveh and Tyre, Hiroshima and Nagasaki. And, as I speak, starvation's specter haunts Berlin and Calcutta. The death of the soul, creeping spiritual paralysis, has its fatal grip on the black-marketers and profiteers, who by their greed condemn others to death.

He advocates *la Résistance* indirectly by alluding to the Spartans' defiance in front of Philip of Macedonia's threat to crush them and Torquemada who led the Inquisition. In "The meaning of the Cross," he shows the power of forgiveness in staging a young nurse healing an officer who had been her torturer and that of her family during the Armenian atrocities. In "Essentials of happiness," he gives as an example of trust in God two nuns walking around, under the Bombing of the Blitz of London, carrying food to children.

He speaks against the Holocaust and against German romanticism in a reference to Bismarck putting some flowers into a little girl's hand and yet wanting to turn France into pulp ("The Harvest of the Holy Spirit"). He advocates and praises the churches for opposing the death-camps in Germany and the caste system in India ("Why I Believe in the Catholic Church").

The second is racism. Having lived in Africa for 7 years, he naturally took a stand against slavery. In the texture of the sermons there are references to both life and literature. He names William Wilberforce who dared oppose and defeat the slave trade and Michael Scott who fought for the Zulus and the Indians oppressed in Durban, South Africa. He summarizes Alan Paton's *Cry the Beloved Country* to show the sadness and compassion of the two fathers of different racial background weeping over their sons' fighting (A Victorious faith conquering racial prejudice). From the radio or the newspapers, he includes scandals caused by the inconsistency of the church regarding segregation in America and admires modern martyrs like the Presbyterian Robert B. McNeill of Columbus, Georgia, and the Reverend Mr. Fred B. Manthey of the Congregational Church of Levittown, Pennsylvania. Both were removed for preaching integration and took their downfall with courage.

Thirdly, other contemporary references in the sermons touch social issues: the improvement of prisons by Elizabeth Fry and of working conditions for small boys by Charles Kingsley in "Why I Believe in the Catholic Church"; the struggle of racist Governor Long of the State of Louisiana whilst trying to implement social programs for the schools and the poor in "Victorious faith conquering Skepticism"

Finally he uses biographical references as examples, foils or consolations. In "Saints alive," he presents a rainbow of saints from Francesco Bernadone, Francis of Assisi and Thomas Aquinas, to John Bunyan and John Woolman. In "The divinity of our Lord" he contrasts Mohammed and Buddha to Jesus in physical and mental strength. In "The meaning of the Resurrection today" he endeavors to console the congregation for the loss of young casualties, by referring to the famous Mozart, Schubert and Keats, who all died young, but lived full lives, with meaning and purpose.

Logic

Sermons, by their nature are mostly argumentative. They appeal to reason in order to provoke action. Apart from the usual pattern of Doctrine, Reason and Use, common to all Puritan sermons, Davies uses logic to compare and contrast as well as categorize in explicative discourse. "God's Covenant with men" spends much time explaining the word covenant by analogy with contract and agreement, and most of the sermon is argumentative. In "The meaning of the Cross" he dwells on the similarities and the contrasts between Judaism, Islam and Christianity, and opposes, by quoting Dorothy Sayers, a ludicrously superficial to a deeper view of Christianity. In "The Severity of God," he uses logical arguments to show why people should come to church on a regular basis. This may be one of his rare moments when he uses invective, considering absenteeism as "blasphemy," at the same time as gentle humor, disclaiming that he is ONLY begging for his salary. "Essentials of happiness" gives four recipes for a good conscience in prescriptive order and within each category, there is a list of advice. Finally "Christianity as the Servant Church" deviates from the usual pattern of doctrine, reason and use to denounce the major changes in the twentieth century both in art and in religion and attempt to correlate the two.

Let us take as an example "Why I Believe in the Holy Catholic Church." The sermon starts with objections to the church. It starts with 1.) The reality of the church: criticism of the church; why indeed have a church at all; religion is private, but it is also corporate; the failures and successes of the church; hypocrisy in the church; concluding with reform the church from inside. Then Davies delineates 2.) The ideal church: as divine society; as undivided society despite the schisms, beyond space and time; as a holy society of redeemed and dedicated men and women.

Rhetoric and Imagery

Sermons, to appeal to the congregation in a twenty minute span or so, need to be wrought with rhetoric and imagery; so we find references to classical lore, many historical references to the past, church history, and the contemporary; his examples are taken out of the Bible or out of life to illustrate his points. Scenes are particularly vivid, as one might expect of someone who took art as a full-time occupation during much of his retirement. Because of his imagination both examples and scenes sometimes become interesting dramatizations, of which there is less of a sample here, but which are even more obvious in two series called *Jesus Monarch of Men* and in the *Cross-examination* sermons.

Rhetoric

To appeal to a mixed audience, the logical progression is often carefully dressed in rhetoric and craftsmanship. Because Davies adheres to the plain style, there are very few, if any, allegories, personifications, metonymies or periphrases; because of the compassion of his tone and clarity of message, there are few examples of figures of substitution like antiphrasis, litotes, or euphemisms or of omission like ellipses. On the other hand figures marking opposition and figures designed to amplify and insist abound. We find parallelisms and antitheses, anaphora and repetition, enumerations, rhetorical questioning and exclamations, an occasional use of hyperbole and hypothesis, and a plethora of imagery in comparisons, similes and metaphors.

Davies's rhetoric was aimed at being persuasive rather than coercive: parallelism, repetitions and anaphora abound: In "Immortality" we hear:

> Sometimes that judgment comes in History, as it comes today with a rising crescendo of fury, terrible as an army with banners. Sometimes that judgment waits until the Judgment Day of Christ. Sometimes that judgment of God comes in personal life, where the soul has so neglected the spiritual help of Christ and his church, that it is an empty vault, a mask of a face covering sheer emptiness.

In "The Verdict on the Cross" the repetition "You are poor Peter . . . You are poor Judas . . . You are the frightened disciples . . ." is last combined with an antithesis: "You are there and I am here."

In "Wanted a perpetual Pentecost," repetition is mixed with progression and accumulation: "It was an empty church, a church in a graveyard, a church which modernity had left in a backwash of history, building its town in a new quarter, a church of inner darkness, a church of spectators."

And to show that he is aware of the difficulties of the splitting church, we hear in "Why I believe in the Holy Catholic Church": "Well, I can tell you of some of the splits: the Roman Catholics, the Church of England, the Methodists (all three brands of them), the Baptists, the Congregationalists, the Quakers and the Plymouth Brethren."

In "All things work together for those who love God" we find enumeration combined with rhetorical questioning, as if pounding into his flock's hearts:

> Do you love God? Do you love God and serve Him above all other masters; do you love Him more than your own life? Or do you live with one eye on God and the other eye on the main chance? Tonight I am challenging youth in the morning of life; do you love God? I am challenging men and women here in the middle busy years of life; do you love God? I am challenging men and women in the evening of life; do you love God?

To wake up the congregation from its sleep, apostrophe and rhetorical questioning are quite common. It was used by Christ a few times as he asked: "Who do you think I am?" and "Do you love me?" Davies asks in "Saints Alive," "Where is your Rome?"

Sympathetic to the degrees of faith in his parishioners, the preacher often starts his sermons with questions: "What is Christian love? Is it the sense of pity?" ("The harvest of the Holy Spirit") or "Why did Jesus come to earth? ("Essentials of happiness") or "Is the Christmas story a lovely legend? Or is it eternal truth?" ("The Incarnation").

Questions and oppositions are shot at the listener in the hope to elicit an inner response before stating the truth. In "Sin is rebellion against God," Davies attempts to put some backbone into the usually bland view that sin is only psychological error. He asks about the concept of Original Sin, inherited from the mother's womb: "An extravagance? An attempt to shift the blame? A refuge in talk of heredity and environment? No, a deep perception of spiritual truth."

There is no pussyfooting in Davies's sermons, but clear definition as to what he saw as the truth. Antitheses can be flippant as in "I Believe in the Holy Catholic Church" when the preacher affirms, as he admits the shortcomings and dissentions and the occasional cruelty in and perpetrated by the Christian church: "I believe in the Holy Catholic church and I regret that it does not exist."

Speaking of the effect the Saints of the church have on us in "Victorious faith conquering Skepticism" he expresses ambiguity: "We are attracted by what contradicts us most. But this is only half the truth. The other half is that we are condemned by what contradicts us most. St. Francis, Dr. Schweitzer, and supremely their Lord and ours, shame us, humble us."

The sermon "Christianity as the Servant Church" is particularly resonant with oppositions, as Davies tries to show the evolution of the church for the needs of the modern world. Describing Christ as the man for others, Davies states: "He is not the pre-existent Christ but the pro-existent Christ." Defining the social role of the church, we hear: "It is to be a holy secularity, not set apart, but sent serving into secularity" and later, according to Gibson Winter, it is neither a "cultic organism … nor a confessional fortress … but … a prophetic fellowship."

Questioning can occasionally become hypothesis to convince the unbeliever. In "The Hidden God," Davies has to defend to a stricken congregation the choice of God to give us free will to do good or bad. To the question: "Why doesn't God intervene and stop the war?" he retorts: "Suppose God had chosen the former way: then there would be no moral evil in the world … But what would be the value of such service, when the creature who gave it was not free to do otherwise?" But this is a rare occurrence.

What is not rare is the use of exclamation as a way to reach the heart in assent or indignation. In "Immortality" Davies expresses the liberation brought by the assurance of immortality in these terms:

> It is the eternal home-coming! What are twenty, thirty, forty, fifty, sixty, seventy, eighty years compared with eternity! What is liberation from the evil clutches of the Gestapo, compared with liberation from death, the last enemy that shall be destroyed in our passing hence! Death is abolished, liquidated, annihilated by the Resurrection of Jesus Christ … What great glory to God!

In "A victorious faith conquering racial prejudice," exclamation is used as irony. Color-blindness in a country with racial tensions like Africa or the America of the fifties and sixties is viewed thus by its detractors: "This is revolutionary! Crush it! Away with troublemakers! Crucify them! These are they that have turned the world upside down!"

Illustrations and Examples

Davies was convinced that the only thing most people remembered in a sermon was the illustration, hence his care in choosing examples and coining imagery. He refers to musicians, but analyses paintings. He admired the luminosity of Rembrandt's paintings and speaks of his *Ecce Homo* in the anecdote of a little girl who challenged the master. As he expressed his admiration for the sacrifice of Christ and she realized the profound gratitude of the painter, she asked him bluntly what he had done for Him. This, tradition says, was the origin of the famous painting. This, Davies argues, is the question one should ask all Christians.

There are also two references to Raphael whom he liked for a different kind of luminosity, that of the Italian sky. One is to the paintings in the rooms of the Vatican. The other mixes description and drama. In "Lord I believe, help my unbelief" Davies first depicts Raphael's painting of Christ healing the epileptic boy, with its human drama, to contrast it with the peace of the mountain of the Transfiguration. Then, to make the picture come to life, he dramatizes the dialogue between the humble and worried father and the healing Jesus. There are other references to visual art, as in "Saints alive," a reference to stained-glass windows and MGM pictures. In "Christianity as a Servant Church" he goes over the gamut of changing fashions in art from post-impressionism to "Op" art and proceeds to correlate art and religion.

Examples are taken out of the Bible, of history, literature or real life. He correlates the learned to everyday life, and human experience to the biblical testimony. For instance in "The Harvest of the Holy Spirit," in a discourse of the three forms of love, Eros, Philia and Agape, he explains Eros by the statue erected on Piccadilly Circus.

Further human and humorous instances include in "Why I Believe in the Holy Catholic Church" the anecdote taken from Victor Murray, when a schoolboy expresses pride in his school, but confesses that he is a bad representative, or in the same sermon, the story of the poor man who is promised a crown in England and would prefer the modest sum of half a crown in the immediate present, with the pun on the word "crown."

In "Immortality" he uses quid pro quo to lighten the mood in the time of war:

> The story is told that an American soldier was walking along Whitehall. He had only recently arrived in London and it was therefore unfamiliar to him. He saw a British colonel approaching in his red hat. Undaunted he asked him: "Which side is the War Office on?" The Colonel's eyes twinkled as he gave the laconic reply, "On our side I hope."

In "The severity of God," there is the story of the old lady who thought that her friend knocking at the door in love was the owner come to collect her rent, to show the fear that people have of letting God into their lives, and that he might take over. There is the story of Bishop Quayle preaching about "trust in God," but incapable of letting go of his daily worries and go to sleep at night. And there is the little girl who gives an ethical lesson to Rembrandt. Other prominent examples have already been dealt with.

Imagery, Metaphors and Similes

Besides these stories we find also an amazing number of images and metaphors drawn from all areas of life. Some are expected: the Holy Spirit as a bird, for instance; but most are vivid. Many are taken from nature, many are mixed metaphors.

In "The Harvest of the Holy Spirit" he uses a scatological image to show the cleansing of Christ: "see Him turn the cesspool of Corinth into a well of water undefiled. A church of God in Corinth, it was like creating a Christian community out of the brothels of Paris!" Or he can be gruesome as in "Wanted a perpetual Pentecost": "Without the presence of the Spirit of God, in the souls of members, the church becomes a human museum, a collection of stuffed-human beings, dead." In "The meaning of the Resurrection" he states: "It would be blasphemous for me to think of the Ruler of the Universe as a giant Hooper, impersonally conveying the carcasses of humanity to the great refuse-heap of time."

His images can be unusual either because of their coining or their application. In "Sin is rebellion against God," we read that these words seem "as remote as old rusty Roman coins, or a Victorian penny-farthing, or a fossil." Later he uses an image from apparel: "He has confessed his sin as he might acknowledge the color of his socks or the size of his hat," to show the levity with which sin is taken in the psychologist's world. In "Wanted, a perpetual Pentecost" he speaks of the desiccated souls of men with a mixed death metaphor: "They are pressed petals in a botanist book, preserved fruits bottled in a dark larder." And in "The Verdict," the bereaved are "barricaded behind the door of fear." Of Christ he uses a colloquial metaphor: "Jesus did not seem to have bees in his bonnet," we read in "The Divinity of our Lord."

The way between death and life is described in coruscating fashion. In "The meaning of the Cross" the weather image is brought forth as a storm:

> Have you ever been on a hill-top in a storm? Once I was. The black cumulus clouds were piling up, filling the valley below me with darkness. The landscape soon was blotted out; the sky and land were deep in mourning, and the wind whistled and shrieked like a soul in pain. But suddenly, for an instant, the clouds parted, and a golden arrow of sunlight broke through the dense darkness.

Introduction

> The Cross is like that. At history's darkest point, there breaks forth history's most blinding light. Where sin abounds, grace does much more abound. The occasion of man's blackest crime and deepest degradation, reveals the blazing wonder of God's holy, forgiving, and reconciling love.

And in "Terminus becomes tunnel" we visualize:

> The impenetrable curtain dividing the end of this life from the inscrutable mystery beyond has been drawn back for an instant. Christ's crimson sunset on Calvary followed by the midnight of human hopes, has been succeeded by a resplendent dawn. A full-stop had become a comma; a terminus becomes a tunnel; in the very centre of the black wall of death there opens the golden-gate and out of it walks the prince of life.

Consolation can be found in remembering the past and that way was always rocky. In "The harvest of the Holy Spirit" he uses another image from nature:

> Time, like a dim haze, softens the rugged features of the landscape, so that even the jagged edges of a rock seen in midsummer seem smoother than they are. We must not let the mists of the centuries blind us to the terrific problems that the first Christian community had to face, how jagged were its rocks. Nor must we forget how the Holy Spirit produced terrific fruits of love in them, enabled them, like pioneers, to surmount the jagged precipice to achievement.

In "Wanted, a perpetual Pentecost" and in "Saints alive" he appeals to the army of the soldiers of Christ: the first martial metaphor unites the faith of judgment with the faith of forgiveness for those who are trying to divorce Christianity from Judaism: "Everyone of them had given himself up to Christ up to the hilt" and "We have the marching orders in the Ten Commandments." The latter, drawn from animal imagery, describes the swarm of underground Christians trying to gain Rome to their cause: "Christianity's attempt to gain this citadel must have been like the attempt of mosquitoes to subdue a lion." In "Terminus Becomes Tunnel" there is a vision of the great and final battle, a reference to Revelation, not unrelated to the hopes of the allied armies of the time:

> The Home of the Caesars and the Church of Christ are locked in a death-grapple. The mailed fists of Nero and Domitian are smashing their way through the dreams of the saints. Here you have the second Babylon, mother of all the abominations of the earth, drunk with the blood of the friends of Jesus, laughing in the intoxication of her tri-

umph, shrieking with fiendish laughter to see the poor pathetic body of Christ being crushed and mangled and battered out of existence. That is what the author of Revelation sees over his shoulder as he writes. What will he say? Will he write: "The battle is lost? Our cause is ruined. There is only one thing to do, which is to sue for mercy." Does he write this? No. He writes: "Hallelujah! Babylon is fallen, is fallen." And why? At the back of the visible world, behind all his pomp and pride and power, he had seen something which Caesar had never seen, something that spelt the doom of Caesar and of all tyranny; he saw a throne up reared above the earth and, sitting on the right hand of the throne of God, the risen and reigning Christ.

And yet Davies insists that the battle is not won for ever. In "Wanted..." Davies uses a nautical image to show the demise and rebirth of the church. It is depicted as an old ship lying down in the shipyard on the Clydebank in Scotland, a place familiar to Davies who had worked many summers as a purser on the Clyde steamers. Revamped, the vessel sails the seas again. Then the Christian church becomes a flotilla of ships, according to each denomination, to serve, as he is called in "Terminus becomes tunnel," "Christ the explorer," who fulfills God's offerings in his covenant with men by three alliterating words: "power, pardon and peace."

Life, for Davies, can only be expressed in poetry, as in hymns and vivid images. He says: "Life is a rare poem from a foreign land" in "The Divinity of our Lord." He uses his eyes as a painter both for description and evocation of living tableaux: such as a vivid portrait of Jesus's physical appearance or showing Christ in action. In "The living union of Christ and his disciples" we see Jesus ambling along the dark streets and entering the precinct of the Temple Court. Then follows symbolic scenery: "gleaming in the light of the full moon was the great Golden Vine that trailed over the Temple Porch..." In "The Harvest of the Spirit" Davies describes the ruby-red love of Christ: "What was this new love? It was a love such as was exhibited by our Lord, a deep, constant, sacrificial love for the sons and daughters of men, love with the blood-red stamp of cross upon it." The image is contrasted to the simplicity of the followers, by the use of simple phraseology: "The disciples and the apostles knew that God was always like that."

Finally one has to sense the rhythm of Davies's prose, at times, not unlike that of the Baptist preachers. In "Why I Believe in the Catholic Church" we hear the quick pace of the conquering church:

> More facts also amaze me about the church. It stretches across space; it stretches across time. Its mighty span reaches across the five continents. It embraces the pale-faced Eskimo in his igloo and the swarthy

African in his kraal. There is in Christ no East or West; no North nor South.

And in "Victorious faith conquering prejudice" one could almost hear Martin Luther King in the delivery of the force of his convictions:

> When my brother for whom Jesus Christ died, suffers insults, and the Jews and the Negroes and Africans are the races that Christians (so-called) have insulted most in the modern world, when my white brethren who are suffering for Christian color-blindness are jailed or have heart-attacks or are kicked out of the ministry, I am insulted; but more, this nation is insulted and supremely God is insulted.

And:

> Next time, recall Jesus was a Jew, Paul was a Jew, Peter was a Jew, Einstein was a Jew, Ann Frank was a Jew, and Arthur Miller is a Jew.

I BELIEVE

LORD, I BELIEVE, HELP MY UNBELIEF

Immediately, the father of the child cried out and said:
"I believe; help my unbelief."

—Mark 9:24

I WISH you could see a famous picture by the Italian master Raphael. It would preach a more memorable sermon on this text than I can. It depicts a great contrast. On one side of the canvas, it shows the mountain of Transfiguration, with our Savior on its summit surrounded by an area of light; on the other side and below on the plain a confused concourse of people, like sheep without shepherd, wrangling and arguing amongst one another; a motley assembly of bystanders of Scribes and Pharisees, disciples and bystanders. In the midst is a man grievously anxious, trying to control his son who is in the midst of a convulsive fit.

Convert the static oil-painting into a moving picture and you see our Savior descending in to the center of the world's confusion and healing the boy possessed by a demon. But first hear their conversation: the boy's father and Jesus translated into modern terms:

Jesus seeing the disputants asks: What are you discussing so hotly? What is the point at issue?

> *The man:* It's like this, sir. I've really come to see you about my epileptic son; something is torturing him badly; sometimes he cannot speak; sometimes, he foams at the mouth and seems to snarl just like a wild animal; and sometimes after one of these fits, he's left limp and lifeless. I brought him first of all to your assistants and asked them to cure him. But they couldn't.
>
> *Jesus to the crowd:* You skeptical people! I haven't much longer to remain in your midst. Will you never learn the lesson of faith? Bring the boy to me.
>
> As they brought him, he was again seized by a fit and dropped to the ground, foaming.

Jesus to the father: Has he been like this for long?

The Father: Ever since he was a youngster. It's been very dangerous; it made him throw himself into the fire and into the river; just as if he wanted to kill himself. But if you can do anything about it, take pity on us and help us.

Jesus: If you have complete faith in me, anything is possible.

The father immediately cried in reply: Lord I believe; help my unbelief.

With the story as a whole, I am not concerned; I want to direct your thoughts to this honest reply of the boy's father: "**Lord, I believe; but help my unbelief.**"

These words show that a struggle was going on in the man's soul for certainty against the ever-present forces of doubt and unbelief. His cry is the cry of everyman confronted by the obstacle to belief. It is your cry.

I. First consider the words: "**help my unbelief.**" That is your problem, isn't it? **Facing doubts.**

My first piece of advice is to do as this man did. Don't pretend that you can believe everything, if you cannot. Don't make believe that doubts aren't there. That will have no better effect than pulling the bedclothes over your head when you hear a strange noise in the house at night. The fact is that you will go on listening for it even when it isn't there. You will still keep wondering what it is, and your fear will become more intense, until in the end, you have to get up and investigate. It would have been far better to do this at the beginning. Remember, whatever doubts you may have had, others have experienced them before you and come through to a stronger faith. Christianity stands by the truth that makes us free and it is not a shame-faced impostor, who must hide his head in the corner. If it is the truth, then it can stand up to criticism.

Christianity calls for no pretense but for honesty. As the principal of Richmond College, Dr. E.S. Waterhouse says: "Our religion calls us to believe, but never to make-believe." In this judgment he was following our Master who realized the sheer honesty of the confession of our text. How easily he, the father of the boy, could have pretended that he believed entirely; it would have been so convenient because then Jesus, he must have thought, would have cured the boy without hesitation. But no, honesty dictated a wiser policy.

The first thing, I say, is: Face up to your doubts. I think that doubts are not only a sign of honesty in our thinking, but they show that our faith is not a dead thing of tradition, but a rediscovered, vital experience. So much for honest doubt and our duty to face it.

But there are also the wrong kinds of doubts: Doubts are sinful if they are of these two kinds. First they are sinful if they are the result of mental laziness which prevents us from thinking things through as far as we can. To love God with your whole mind is not to exaggerate the evil in the world, but to admit the good in it as well. Secondly, the worst kinds of doubts are those which are a defense we have set up, to prevent the invasion of God into some parts of our lives. If we want to deal honestly with our doubts, we must ask ourselves unflinchingly: "Is this doubt that I have an excuse for not facing up to God? Is God making some demand on me which I will not stand up to? Is he requiring me to put something right that is wrong in my relationship to someone else? Is he asking me to undertake some sacrifice which I am not prepared to make? Or am I trying to avoid tackling a habit that I know ought to be dealt with? Intellectual doubts are often produced by moral failures. This is all part of the process of facing up to your doubts: "**my unbelief.**"

Doubts demand honesty. Doubts demand hard thinking. Doubts demand to be faced in the right attitude. The right way is to say: "We will hold to a thing until it is proved false; not, I will not believe a thing until it is proved true."

I want to be as practical as I can and to suggest some thoughts that may help you to pray "LORD, HELP MY UNBELIEF" with some sincerity.

Remember in the first place, even if you doubt some things, there are others you can be quite certain of. Some people say rather loosely that they don't believe in anything any longer. I quote the words of the Reverend Leslie Tizard:

> Something has gone up in smoke somewhere, and the pall is hanging over everything. So they assume that the whole structure of faith is going to pieces in the ruins, whereas, if they took the trouble to look into the matter, they would find that although a part of the building is in flames, the rest is sound enough, at the worst, a little blackened and salvable.

If doubt, that shadow, crosses the sunlight of your faith, it's a very useful thing to sit down, take out pencil and paper; then write down all that you have to thank God for. Remember everything beautiful you have seen: in art galleries, out in the fields or by the sea, in books, in theatres or in picture houses. Put down also all the kindnesses, the unexpected favors you have received, all the examples of bravery and goodliness you have come across. You will find that by this time, you have exhausted all the spare paper in the house and burnt your cooking or missed a train. The moral of this is: there is so much to be thankful for. You had forgotten it before, because you were looking at the world with dark spectacles. Once you took them off and looked back down the vistas of your memory, you saw the truth in perspective. These things of beauty were real experiences and no amount of evil in the world can deny them.

If the problem of evil demands that you banish God from the world of your thought, the problem of good will just as easily demand that you bring him back in order to explain that.

Secondly our faith needs fellowship to sustain it. It is wise to remember that our faith is very much at the mercy of our moods; even the most muscular and robust Christians sometimes lose faith in God when they are passing through a sorrow that seems hard to bear. And when doubt bandages your eyes, it is wise to remember that there are others who can see the brightness. It is good to know that if the sun has gone out for us, there are still others who can see its resplendent radiance. And of course, we gather in church, not only to meet with others who have a radiant confidence in God, but we meet for fellowship with the ever-living son of God. That is the chief source of faith.

The father of the epileptic boy cried: "Lord, I believe," of that much we are certain. He could trust Jesus. Consider all the shadows that crossed our Savior's life: poverty, disappointment, loneliness (at one time even desertion by God), suffering, death. What a series of darknesses! But he could trust. Fellowship with him in the darkness will bring back our faith. Remember:

> Christ leads me through no darker rooms
> Than he went through before;
> He that into God's kingdom comes
> Must enter by this door.

My last word is: prove your faith in action: Whilst Jesus told his disciples to believe in him, his other word was "Follow me." When we are in a mood that makes religion seem hopelessly unreal, it is very useful to do some quite simple act which takes us out of ourselves. What it is does not much matter: going to see someone who is lonely; taking a handful of flowers to someone who is ill; reading to an invalid; looking after the children while a harassed mother goes out shopping; digging a neighbor's garden. Indeed, anyone of the thousand little acts of human kindness will do. If we go out determined that we shall not return until we have done something for somebody, the world and everything in it will look different when we return.

Lord, I Believe, Help My Unbelief

Let me just repeat the stages of the journey by which you can defeat doubt. First, face them honestly. Secondly, ask yourself whether your doubts are not a defense you are putting up to save the necessity of obeying God's call. Thirdly, write down all the beautiful experiences you have been through and all the kindnesses you have received. Fourthly, when your eyes are bandaged, meet with others whose eyes are open and especially meditate on the Light of the Word and remember the shadows of life. Then, leave introspection and go out to prove the reality of goodness by your own sympathetic action.

And pray at all times: "Lord I believe." Thank God for all you can believe; and pray humbly as one who wishes to receive further light: "Help my unbelief."

A VICTORIOUS FAITH: CONQUERING SKEPTICISM

G. K. CHESTERTON once said: "An age chooses as its saint the man who contradicts it most."

This was by way of arguing that the industrialists of the Victorian age who had covered England and America with their "dark Satanic mills" were attracted by Francis, the lover of Nature, who sang of Brother Sun; that those who rapaciously grasped only for prosperity and more prosperity were strangely attracted to God's little poor man who founded an order dedicated to poverty and simplicity. By the same token our age has accorded the highest respect to Albert Schweitzer. In an age of specialism, he combines brilliance in music, medicine, with the single dedication to lifting the life of the humblest of humanity, the African. We are attracted by what contradicts us most. But this is only half the truth.

The other half is that we are condemned by what contradicts us most. St. Francis, Dr. Schweitzer, and supremely their Lord and ours, shame us, humble us, and reveal the easy compromises and complacencies that hitherto satisfied us. A bland poet cried: "We needs must love the highest when we see it." But they crucified the highest when they saw him.

If there are saints that fascinate and contradict us, there are also saints that seem nearer to us, more like us, who mirror our problems: lesser saints who can lead us to the higher saints, and to the King of Saints, Christ. Such is Doubting Thomas; for, as we look at him, we see ourselves. I do not think that any age has had to contend with such religious difficulties as our own: I do not think any of the Christian centuries needs Thomas as badly as we do. The tremendous and rightful advance of the natural sciences, and the applications of the techniques of natural science to the social sciences, have made faith another word for credulity and love only the crude satisfaction of a biological need. "Take nothing on trust" say our new masters the scientists; it is the refusal to accept old hypotheses and the demand for demonstrative proof that brought progress through Newton and through Einstein. It is the very spirit of Thomas. "This theory of the Resurrection of my crucified leader is all very well" he might say say in our language, "but I want visual proof, and tactile demonstration. Let me just put my finger in the wounds and the nail-prints to be sure that this is really Jesus. I want reality, not rumor." That is the scientific spirit. And that is why for a scientific time, faith is so very difficult.

Of course there are many answers to this problem, which I can only mention in passing.

(1) The scientist also has his faith, his underlying unproven and unprovable assumptions to his entire enterprise. He assumes the rationality of the universe, that his mind and other human minds are part of the order which he finds in the world, and which alone make his descriptions and predictions and experiments possible. This might be a uniform illusion; it might equally be truth. There's no way of proving or disproving it. It has to be assumed. That is faith.

(2) Secondly, I might point out that the scientist accepts as true and important aspects of reality factors in our human life which cannot be measured in any accurate quantitative way. Take the very quest for knowledge: for some it is a raging, unquenchable thirst; for others it is a merely nominal thing. There is no index of the thirst for knowledge. Take those emotions that play such a large part in our life: love and hate, anxiety and assurance. Love ranges from the sheer Himalayan heights of the Incarnation where sacrifice flings itself down for the utterly undeserving's sake, to the wallowing pig's trough of lust, with some many intermediate stages. Hate ranges all the way from self-disgust to the calculated genocide of which Ann Frank was a cruel victim. Anxiety stretches from a foolish worry about, let us say, whether we look respectable at a social function, to the neurotic obsession of a Governor Long that the whole of the administration of the State of Louisiana is in league against him. Assurance ranges from the certainty of love to the intolerable cockiness of the self-made man who worships his maker. These cannot be measured, cannot be predicted but they are really there, grandly real or sordidly real. The belief in God and the balance of faith and the direction they give are every bit as genuine a part of the human enterprise as space satellites.

What I want to concentrate our thoughts on is not just that the scientist has faith or even that his impressive picture of the world is only part of it. It is rather that there are two kinds of skepticism, which I shall call dishonest and honest doubt. I think every man who calls himself an agnostic, that is, one who isn't sure about God, ought to inquire very seriously whether his doubts are motivated by a desire to know God and serve him (that, I call honest doubt) or whether he secretly hopes that he will find convincing arguments to disprove God, to laugh at other Christians as fools, and thus be left alone to make hay while the sun shines (that, I call dishonest doubt).

A Victorious Faith: Conquering Skepticism

I believe that the plague of our age is doubting for doubting's sake. I would like to quote the words of Katherine Mansfield, an imaginative genius who died young, written in a letter shortly before her death:

> I am so sick of all this modern seeking which ends in seeking. Seek by all means. But the text goes on "and ye shall find." Of course there can be no ultimate finding. There is a kind of ultimate finding by the way which is enough, is sufficient. But these seekers in the looking-glass, these half-female frightened writers of today—you know, they remind me of the green-fly in roses, they are a kind of blight.

The novelist was right: there is a kind of blight in the world of thought which is sentiment, dramatizing oneself as a superior kind of person who prefers wandering and wondering to finding and believing. It was another genius, and scientist, Blaise Pascal who said:

> There are only two kinds of people who can be called reasonable: those who serve God with all their hearts because they know Him; and those who seek Him with all their hearts because they do not know Him yet.

The difference between dishonest and honest doubt has been superbly dramatised in two novels that appeared about seventy years ago, when the struggle between revelation and scientific reason was at its height. The first is the American novelist, Harold Frederic and his book *The damnation of Theron Ware, or Illumination*. Its subtitle might be Dishonest Doubt. The hero or villain of the story is a Methodist minister of good intelligence, poor education, and a searing ambition, put down in a backwoods parish among a group of sincere but narrow Christians. The novelist contrasts the venerable elders of Methodism, those giants of the frontier who were men of faith and courage, who lived the frugal, compassionate lives of their Master, and did not know where to lay their heads, circuit riders of Christ. He contrasts them with the conceit and vanity of this ministerial puppy. He finds the morning newspaper more important than the Bible; he eagerly devours the latest rationalist literature and prides himself on his superiority to his unlearned congregation.

As his faith weakens, so does his sense of obligation. It is now his wife who is unworthy of him and he throws her off in a rude approach to Celia, a Titianesque female, who gabbles about the higher "gospel" of the Greeks, which she interprets as the life of the senses, of unrestrained freedom, actually license. I will not "trouble" you with the stages of his fall nor with the irony that it is simple-hearted Methodist layfolk who rescue him from degradation. But when the book ends, we see him taking a train for the State of Washington, imaging the crowds spellbound by the speeches of the future Senator for Washington, arrogant to the last peroration!

The moral is clear: let a man cultivate doubts for their own sake, and however noble his calling, released from the ultimate commitment to God and his neighbor, he is only an intelligent beast. The only point in having a mind, like having a mouth, is to close it on something solid: the meat of the Gospel.

The other novelist, Mrs. Humphry Ward, wrote *Robert Elsmere*, out of a profound belief that faith becomes firmly based after undergoing the purification of honest doubt. She gives the agonising story of how an Oxford don leaves his college to become the Vicar of a Southern English church, and there, although no man is more assiduous in caring for his parishioners, educating their children, fighting their landlord for improved housing, and praying for them in their sorrows. Yet he finds it impossible to repeat the creed of the church because he cannot accept it or many parts of it. In the end, like the honest man he is, he looks for a church with the image of the purely human Christ, not the eternal Son of God, but the son of man, the model and mirror of compassion. He links himself with a group of Unitarians who are engaged in settlement work in the teeming slums of industrial London. He organizes a new society, a new Company of Jesus.

This was a deeply practical religion; much of it seems shallowly liberal by our own standards of today and in comparison with classical Christianity. But at one point Elsmere showed genius. He transformed the midday meal in the workman's cottage into a simple sacrament. Let me read you a description of the noon meal in the carpenter's home:

> Inside was a curious sight. The table was spread with the midday meal. Round the table stood four children, the eldest about fourteen and the youngest six or seven. At one end of it stood the carpenter himself in his working apron, brawny ... bowed a little by his trade. Before him was a plate of bread, and his horny hands were resting on it ...
>
> Something in the attitude of all concerned reminded me, kept me where I was silent.
>
> The father lifted his right hand.
>
> "The Master said, **Do this in remembrance of Me!**"
>
> The children stooped for a moment in silence. Then the youngest said slowly, in a little softened cockney voice that touched me extraor-

dinarily, "**Jesus, we remember Thee always.**" It was the appropriate response.

Robert Elsmere had to rethink the traditional faith, as his honesty required him to do, but he was satisfied with no mere negations or denials.

So my advice is two-fold. First see whether those doubts are honest or dishonest. If they are dishonest, then there is nothing that can be done until God, by some tragedy in your life, shows you the superficiality of materialism. If there is also the least admixture of honest doubt, then the true response is: "Lord I believe, help Thou my unbelief." Build upon the faith you have, use all the means of grace: the Bible as the record of God's gracious dealings with men, the encouragement of friends who have been humble enough to put their hands in the hand of God, the lives of the great servants of God, and the greatest of all Christian services, which God is to share, the Communion.

I BELIEVE IN GOD THE FATHER ALMIGHTY

THE HIDDEN GOD

Verily Thou art a God that hidest thyself.
—Isaiah 45:15

Belief in God is easy when the sun is shining, but not when the blinds in the house are all drawn. Sorrow, misfortune, pain come and we cry: "Where is God?" He is hidden, or so it seems to us, and we say in despair: "Verily thou art a God that hidest thyself."

We feel this doubly so in war-time. Twenty-five years ago saw the close of a world catastrophe, the Great War, with its ten million dead and its four years of mental and physical agony. Where was God then? Where is God today? Did H. G. Wells speak for the majority when he said: "If I thought there was a God who looked down on battles and death.... able to prevent these things ... I would spit in His empty face"?

I. Why God Hides Himself

(1) His purposes are greater than our imaginings. He is the high and holy One dwelling in light unapproachable. His ways are higher than our ways; his thoughts than our thoughts. God is perfect holiness and we have sinned against the light.

(2) Because of his respect for human personality, he will not thrust himself upon men. If he did, he would undo his own work in us: he would take from us the most precious thing that we have—our freedom of choice and will.

In the creation of man two possibilities were open to God. He could bring into being a creature whose every thought and action were determined by the divine will; or he could give him a will of his own.

Suppose God had chosen the former way: then there would be no moral evil in the world: no greed, no lust, and no war. Man would always live uprightly and honestly, serving his fellows and obeying his God. But what would be the value of such service, when the creature who gave it was not free to do otherwise? Men would be marionette dolls in the hand of Omnipotence. No, there would be no virtue in goodness if it were not the result of man's own free choice. What light does this throw on the war?

I am often asked: "Why doesn't God intervene and stop the war?" The answer is that having made man as he is, God will not mar his own creation, by taking away the power of choice. If man by his ignorance, folly and sin, turns this world into a hell then he cannot blame God for it; he has only himself to blame for it. God hides himself because of his respect for our freedom.

(3) God hides himself that our powers may develop and grow. If he hides himself when we suffer, it is only that through pain we may come to maturity; that patience and bravery may be born; that we may become strong.

A modern writer tells of a man whose wife was an invalid. For some time, he had been accustomed to carrying her about the house, but all his attentions only encouraged her to pander to her weakness. One day he discovered this. He realized that she must exert her own powers, that she would never be strong if she leaned on his support. It was difficult to refuse to carry her; it was still more difficult to stand aside and watch her painful, stumbling attempts to walk. But his restraint meant her development. So, also, God hides himself that we may develop our own powers.

II. Though God Is Hidden, He Is Not Absent

He has not flung the world into space and then left it to take its own course. He is quite near to us, because he has come to us, hidden, but hidden in the form of a man. That is what the Incarnation means that God came down in hidden form, in this carpenter of Nazareth, this man Jesus. If the infinite and holy God were to enter this realm of space and time, to draw near to his rebellious children, he must hide himself in the form of a man. The Christian Gospel is the Good News that this has happened. The hidden God has come near to us in his Son: that his Word is spoken to us in Jesus Christ. His is a truth that was born in the experience of those who trod the streets of Palestine with Jesus of Nazareth. It has been authenticated in the lives of men and women since.

Job's question rings across the centuries: can man by searching find out God? The answer is: no, he cannot. God remains for ever hidden from the unaided human reason. But the only begotten Son has declared him. In Christ, God has entered into those very experiences in which we feel he is farthest away. He shared our sorrows and our pain; he shed tears at the news of his friend Lazarus's death. He shared our agony, more than our agony, at the Cross. In death itself where God seems most hidden, at the darkest point of our existence, we see most brightly that God is there. We watch the net closing around him. We stand by the Cross; there evil triumphs, scatters his friends, wrecks his ministry, crushes his life. There the incarnate Son of God dies. Jesus drains the last bitter dregs of the cup of human experience. He too feels that the face of God is hidden. In despair he cries: "My God, my God, why hast Thou forsaken me?" So Jesus felt, yet men have realized that there, more than in all else he did, there was God.

That was how the centurion felt at the Cross. There was the confidence of Christ, commending his soul to his father, in that black hell of despair. His was no hardened or dangerous criminal. The hardened soldier looked, and as he looked, the truth dawned upon him. "Truly" he cried "this was the Son of God."

Darkness will come, even to the Christian, days and nights when God seems far away. Nevertheless, as we stand beneath the Cross of Christ, we know that Faber's words are true:

> Thrice blest is he to whom is given
>
> The instinct which can tell
>
> That God is on the field when He
>
> Is most invisible.

1943

THE GOD OF NATURE AND THE GOD OF GRACE

Harvest Thanksgiving 1943

He left not Himself without witness in that he did good and gave you from heaven rains and fruitful seasons, filling your hearts with food and gladness.

—Acts 14:17 (St. Paul at Lystra)

Why is it that harvest festivals are so popular? I found myself asking this question after a year's ministry among you. Christmas is popular, Easter is popular, Whitsuntide fairly popular. But the peak periods seem to be the Junior Church Anniversary and the harvest festival. Either is a red-letter-day in the Christian year, when we give God thanks for his revelation in the life, death or Resurrection of Jesus Christ. Why should we give thanks more readily at Harvest or at the Junior Church Anniversary?

We shall find the answer in the kind of festival we hold. The Junior Church Anniversary is the festival of the Child; the Harvest is the festival of the Earth. The first reason for their popularity is surely their very obviousness. The drab, grey world in which we live would be immeasurably colder without the warm gaiety of children and their irrepressible good spirits. The aging become Peter Pans in their company. And, whilst we are profoundly grateful for our salvation, we are more obviously grateful for our food. Salvation for most of us is a very abstract thing; food is a substantial need. As Dr. Johnson put it: "The state of the country never yet put any man off his victuals." So we hold a Harvest festival to thank God for the obvious gift of sustenance.

Then a second reason is surely that the Harvest Festival has come to mean so much more to us in war-time. To use St. Paul's phrase we are members one of another.

War-time, because it has made food scarce, has brought home to us its value. We cannot eat the simplest meal of bread and butter or usually margarine without reflecting on the risks that have been taken to bring the wheat across the seas. Our daily bread has come to as not only through the grace of God and the labor of the farmer, but through the gauntlet of submarines and four-engine bombers. Just as our Savior broke the bread of sacrifice at the Last Supper, we are eating the bread of sacrifice at every meal. Yes, and as we think of the hungry pinched faces of starving children in Europe, ransacking dust-bins for the veriest morsel of bread in Belgium or in Greece, we, like the Lord of Life, give thanks before we eat.

Then as Free Church people, I think we have extra joy at harvest-time. We have turned our backs on the ritual of the Roman Church; with its rich riot of color, its rainbow tapestries, hangings and pictures, its begemmed crosses and silver crucifixes, its candles and incense, its stained-glass windows and its banners. Our churches have a simple austerity amounting almost to nakedness for all services except one—the Harvest Festival. And then we allow ourselves to luxuriate in a feast of fragrance and color. Here we are ritualists for a day. Communion-table, pulpit, and window-ledges are more richly decorated, than the highest church, just for today. It is the most colorful service of the year.

These I think are the reasons for the popularity of the Harvest Festival. And, as far as they go, they are good reasons.

The God of Nature

Now we return to the text. Paul and Barnabas had come to Lystra. There they were mistaken for Greek gods and the population, to their embarrassment, fell down and worshipped them. St. Paul immediately pointed out that both he and Barnabas were men of like passions, as they were. They were therefore not worthy of worship. The living God was alone worthy of worship. And to make this point in a way that these simple heathens could understand, St. Paul requested them to give thanks to the God of Nature. He had obviously done something which a mere man like Paul himself could not have done. He had sent them the harvest. "And He left not himself without witness in that He did good, and gave you from heaven rains and fruitful seasons, filling your hearts with food and gladness."

The glorifying of the God of nature was, you will notice, only the first stage in the worship of God. It was as if St. Paul said: "You must have an object of worship. But you can't worship mere men like yourselves. Worship God, the giver who is the Lord of the harvest." It was a counsel to ignorant men making their first halting steps towards God.

I read only this week a profound definition of the four degrees of love given by the great St. Bernard. They are love of self, love of God for man's sake, love of God himself, and finally love of man and all things for God's sake. You will notice that the pagans of Lystra were being invited to the second stage—love of God for man's sake. They were babes and had to feed on milk before they could be given the strong meat of the Gospel.

My point is this: The harvest festival is only the lowest rung on the ladder of adoration. It is commendable in pagans, but it is only the beginning for Christians. It is not very different in quality from the love of the small boy for his aunt—a love of postal-orders, which finds its expression of gratitude in the yearly letter sent to her on his birthday. Of course, it is preferable to sheer ingratitude. But such religion is adolescent, immature.

Moreover, the love of the God of Nature is fraught with difficulties. Does he always appear to be benevolent in his creation? Can you offer up a harvest-thanksgiving in a desert or after a drought? Can you thank God for thistles if they supplant the wheat? Habakkuk could and did: "For though the fig-tree shall not blossom, neither shall the fruit tree be in the vines; the labor of the olive shall fail, and the fields shall yield no meat; the flock shall be cut off from the fold, and there shall be no herd in the stalls: Yet will I rejoice in the Lord, I will joy in the God of my salvation." But Habakkuk's *Te Deum* was only possible because he worshipped the God of his salvation. His God was more than the God of Nature. He was the God of Grace.

The truth is that if we only knew God the Creator, we should not always find him benevolent. And if in our own country we find nature benevolent, should we find it so in the tropics? Aldous Huxley has suggested that Wordsworth could not have been a nature-mystic in the tropics, because there he would have found "nature red in tooth and claw." But even in this country it is possible to stand on Symonds Yat and be aware not of Divine benevolence but of Divine indifference. What was the experience of Paul Elmer More, the distinguished American writer? He thought of the vast destructive forces of nature which had built up the Severn Valley—the convulsions of lava that became mountains, the huge swirling of waters that had scooped out the Severn, centuries before. Then he turned to contemplate the peaceful scene beneath the birds sailing on the seas of air, the gentle stolid ox gazing contentedly:

> To the eye it was a wide-spread theatre of joy and a masque of peaceful beauty. Until I thought of what lay beneath the surface. Here in fact was an army of countless individuals, each driven on by an instinctive lust of life as if engaged on a vast internecine warfare—each blade of grass fighting for its place under the sun and obtaining it by the suppression of some other plant, each animal preying for sustenance upon some other form of life. It is a system of ruthless competition and remorseless extermination.

His verdict on the scene was: "From every spot of the earth rises continually the battle-cry of Nature: *Vae victis.*"

We can worship God when we see the golden corn dancing in the summer sunlight; but can we worship him when we see a snake gliding through the grass towards a hypnotized bird? We can praise him for the lark's glad carol; can we praise him for the bloodthirsty baying of the hounds? We can thank him for the sunshine and rain that drop out of the heavens; can we thank him for the hawk that drops on the field-mouse out of the same sky?

The truth is that we cannot be sure of his benevolence in nature, until we have first seen his benevolence in grace. We can thank him for our creation only after we have seen his re-creation in Christ.

He is supremely known and adored in Grace. In Nature, he may seem capricious, like Nature's own moods. In Christ he is known as Eternal and unchanging Love. In Nature he is seen as absolute Power and infinite Wisdom; in grace alone is he known as invincible Love. In Nature he may appear to be neutral; in Christ he is known to be our ally. In Nature he seems to be remote, austere, dwelling amidst an arsenal of thunderbolts and earthquakes and deluges; in Christ alone, he is near.

At this time of Harvest we shall give him thanks for common gifts: the sunshine and the rain that he pours prodigally upon good and evil alike; we shall bless him for his creation of ourselves and our brothers who through the commonwealth of labor and commerce make available his gifts, by patient and dignified work in the fields, by hazardous enterprises over the ocean, and by distribution at home.

But we shall not forget the uncommon gift, the greatest, which alone makes us Christians, "His unspeakable gift" as St. Paul describes it, admitting the sheer inadequacy of human language to match the gift of Christ with gratitude.

In the words of the General Thanksgiving: "We bless Thee for our creation, preservation, and all the blessings of this life; but, above all for Thine inestimable love in the redemption of the world by our Lord Jesus Christ; for the means of grace, and for the hope of glory."

In Christ we are no longer orphans in the Universe. The God of Nature is seen to be the God of Grace. He is our Father; "He hath not left Himself without witness in that He did good and gave you from heaven rains and fruitful seasons, filling your heart with food and gladness." Yes, but also with Christ the Heavenly Bread and the gladness, which is the good news of the Gospel.

Reference: Pastor Wehrmand, *Language of Love*

THE SEVERITY OF GOD

For we shall all stand before the judgment seat of God . . . So then each one of us shall give an account of himself to God.

—Romans 14:10 and 12

As I read over these words in the virile Letter Saint Paul sent to the church in Rome, I thought of a modern illustration of this parable of judgment. Sutton Vane made a play of it called *Outward bound* and Warner Brothers re-issued it as a film entitled *Between Two Worlds*.

The scene opens in a steamship office in an English port. A small group of people are anxiously awaiting permission for a sea-crossing to the United States. The group includes a swaggering financier, Lindley, an insufferably domineering and browbeating person; a conceited actress; a witty and sarcastic newspaper-reporter who is living with the actress and a little friendly Irish woman of small means. There is also a merchant seaman, a very cheerful rough diamond. Further, a mild gentle elderly man is obviously hen-pecked by his superficial and selfish wife. The last of the number is an amiable but very sensitive clergyman. As they are given their reservations for the boat, a Viennese refugee pleads to be given a reservation, but he has no papers, and cannot leave. The other group gets into taxis and on the way to the docks, their cars receive a direct hit from a bomb.

The unhappy refugee, forbidden his passage, returns to his apartment and there, he and his fiancée turn on the gas and commit suicide. The next scene shows these two and the other group of passengers aboard a ship. They are dead, but they do not realize the fact. They are all sailing on the ship of destiny. In the scenes that follow, we have ample opportunity of taking stock of their characters, of dividing them into sheep and goats. It would spoil your enjoyment of the film if I were to hint how they discover that they are dead. At one point in the film they are told by the steward of the ship that they will have to meet the examiner. He turns out to be another clergyman, one who is the friendly but firm representative of God. How fairly and wisely does he mete out the rewards and punishments?

The financier makes desperate efforts to bribe him and he goes to the hell that he has already created in this life for those he has swindled and oppressed. The actress reveals that she has been unhappy in her life of pretence and sophistication: she gets the second chance at the innocence that she had longed for. The elderly gentle henpecked-man, who has never known a moment of happiness since his bachelor days, returns to the friends of those days of long ago. His money-grabbing snobbish wife gets the imposing castle that she demands from the examiner; but her punishment is to live in it alone for eternity. She will have no opportunities for display or snobbishness, for she will be alone. The merchant seaman, unpretentious, hardworking, good, family-man, also goes to felicity. The sarcastic reporter, who was only sarcastic to hide his fear, needs appreciation and encouragement; he finds it in Mrs. Midget, the humble Irish woman who promises to be his housekeeper. The faithful amiable minister who has labored at dull routine for many years in the same parish and who was taking his first voyage as a well-earned change is given the task of helping the examiner, in fact, of continuing his ministry in a new sphere. The two suicides, who were afraid of life and its responsibilities are sent back again into the world to try life again.

Now hear our text again. "For we shall stand before the judgment-seat of Christ ... so then each one shall give an account of himself."

Judgment is inevitable.

We shall all stand before the judgment-seat of Christ. Throughout the film the passengers are never allowed to forget that they will have to meet the Examiner, the Judge. How wise it would be if we went throughout our life hearing the solemn tolling of the bell of judgment.

I. Judgment is inevitable because it alone gives seriousness and dignity to human life. What kind of a world would it be in which the rapacious financier who sweated his employees and trampled on his colleagues, was allowed to triumph? What kind of a world would it be if the social snob hurt the sensitive and the poor with her taunts in which the social climber and the superficial were allowed to triumph? What kind of a world would it be in which the morally unclean were happy? Such a world would be an insult in the face of God. It would make all the martyrs into fools, all the heroes into nincompoops, all the self-sacrificing into sentimentalists. In their place, the cynics, the cowards, the selfish tyrants, would cry: "We have won. The prizes go to the rich, the powerful, and the ruthless." But it is not so: there is a day of judgment, a day of reckoning. God who knows the secrets of our hearts will not judge us as the world judges. He will not be impressed by bank accounts of magnitude, nor by social success or fame or titles or distinctions. He will ask only one question: "Did you live for me or for yourself?"

The only assets he is interested in are the assets of character. And it will be that question. That will give dignity to the finest human achievements; that will cheer the widow who brought up her family on slender means to love God; that will cheer the man who refused to be bitter when cancer was slowly eating him away; that will cheer all who kept their faith in God when all around were forsaking or ignoring him.

II. The second thing that we must say about the Examiner is that he cannot be tricked. He sees through our deceits and petty evasions. We cannot camouflage our souls from his holy sight. We might as well be clear about that here and now. This very week I realized the futile way that some people try to deceive themselves. I was calling on a house to ask if the people there were ill; it was so long since they had been to church. Do you know what the excuse was? "We expect that in a year or so we shall be leaving the district, we didn't want to become too closely attached to your church and then have to uproot ourselves." That excuse might do for the minister and put him off. But do you think the God of all the earth whose church was bought by the blood of Christ, his Son is mocked, is fooled by such a reply? Men and women, in the sight of God, whom you must one day face, I beseech you remember you have to do with him.

Every part of your Christian life has to be accounted for on the Day of Judgment. Some of you treat the God of Heaven as if he were a poor relation. Those miserly three pennies put in the collection, do you recognize that this is the payment you are making God for the gift of life, for the sacrifice of his only begotten son for your redemption, for your eternal life? Dare you, I repeat, would you dare to put that in the outstretched palm of God if he faced you now? Would you say "This is exactly how much I value you?"

Or, think of next Sunday morning. It is probably bleak, frosty, and foggy. You are some distance away from the house of God. You had an exhausting time the day before. You say: "I'm certainly not going to church this morning, I don't feel up to it." Do you realize that the words are addressed to God? You can't, or you wouldn't attempt to deceive him or yourself. But this God whose command to worship you are ignoring is not asleep or deaf. He hears, and in that unguarded moment, what you are saying in effect is: "God can do without his worship this morning." That is blasphemy, sheer blasphemy, an insult, spitting in the face of God.

I could think of many other insults we offer God, but I will be silent. It is enough if I have made you see that we live every moment under the eye of the Great Taskmaster, and wise are we if we anticipate the Day of Judgment by our own judgment of ourselves. "We shall all stand before the judgment-seat of Christ."

Judgment gives dignity and worth to our life here, makes it a life of training and discipline. Judgment also touches us here and now to see ourselves in the presence of God, without self-deception that we may prepare ourselves for eternal life.

And for that eternal life with him, God gives us the discipline of Christian worship and Christian service of our fellows.

What begins as a duty ends as a delight.

An old lady lived on small means at the top of a four-storied flat. One day she heard a tramp of feet coming up the stairs, approaching her door. Then came the knock on the door. She cowered in a corner. The knocking went on louder and more insistent. She remained crouched, almost paralyzed in the corner. Then a voice shouted: "Mary, this is your friend." Instantly, the old lady ran to open the door. "Oh!" she said, "I did not know it was you. I thought it was the man groveling for the rent."

Many men and women make the same mistake when God tries to take control of their lives, when he knocks at the door of their souls for entrance. They think he demands rent, but he comes as a friend. In the trials, responsibilities and struggles of life, he wears a frown. He is testing us. But in Christ, we know he smiles a welcome.

> Judge not the Lord by feeble sense
>
> But trust Him for his grace
>
> Behind a frowning providence
>
> He hides a smiling face.

Remember that he judges; but that there is no condemnation to them that are Christ's. And so, you have the secret for this life and for that other journey between two worlds.

ALL THINGS WORK TOGETHER

All things work together for good to them that love God.
—Romans 8:28

With those who love God, He cooperates in all things for good.
—Dr. C. H. Dodd

All things must work together for our good, if we love God.
—Søren Kierkegaard

CHARLES LAMB has an essay called "The Two Races of Men." He divides men into those who borrow and those who lend, those who give and those who grab. It is a useful distinction for estimating the value of the lives of men, but less so today, when the government does our giving for us, conscripting our money for causes which we would not uphold sufficiently by our spontaneous giving. Nor is it a good distinction for Christians who cannot take Polonius's advice too seriously: "Neither a borrower nor a lender be," for we know that we are perpetual borrowers from the credit of God. Life salvation, our growth in grace, our fellowship in the church in heaven and earth are already given. And "we love him because he first loved us" from the moment that in Baptism he set his seal upon us, nurtured us in his way in our mother's arms and in the bosom of the church. "By the grace (the free-gift) of God I am what I am" said St. Paul. And we are what we are by the same giving from God and receiving by us.

Leslie Tizard is nearer the truth, I think, when in his book *Facing Life with Confidence* he says: "Men may be divided into those whose general tendency is to try to escape from life and those who stand up to it."

There is no limit almost to the ways that men and women will try to escape from life. Some seek forgetfulness in drinking, in trying to drown their sorrows in unconsciousness. Some one said that in the sordid East End men drink because it's the quickest way out of London.

Some find oblivion in drugs, stifling the sting of life in the anodyne of opium or concentrated saccharine.

Others find their escape in literature, in drama, or in the films, identifying themes with the heroes and heroines of an unreal world who find the success, the fame and the happiness of which they feel they have been cheated.

Some again, shelter behind other persons on whom they can throw the burden of responsibility for any decisions they have to make. A headache or a nervous breakdown may save one from facing up to a difficult situation. At the last there is the "uttermost refuge from reality," suicide. Men and women, we live in the world where all these devices, the most natural and the most desperate, are used to the uttermost.

The urgent question is: "Am I going to face life, or am I going to run away from it? Are you going, as an Army Chaplain put it to his men, to fight it, or funk it?

The Gospel of the love of God has the answer. It is, summed up by St. Paul, in the 28th verse of the eight chapter of the Epistle to the Romans: "All things work together for our good, if we love God."

Did you notice that I have not used the Authorized or Revised version translation? The usual translation is: "All things work for good to them that love God." That would do well enough if people had not misconstrued those words of St. Paul to mean only: "In spite of appearances to the contrary, all's well that ends well." This is not what St. Paul meant. His word, interpreted in this way, sounds as irrelevant as the chirpings of a canary in a concentration camp, remote from life and its hard actualities. But these words are the toiling of a bell, lifted high above a ruined and desolate city, whose tongue is the word of God tolling to bring us back to our truth. They are warning, solemnly warning the sons of men. Their message to a dying world, blinded by its selfishness, rotting in its sins, awaiting the death-blow of the atomic-bomb, is "love God, or die."

This word of God is a conditional: if. You either live as individuals, as families, as communities, or nations, in the love of God, or you perish. You obey my laws, or you disobey them and break yourselves. The signs of the times, the Chairman of the Congregational Union reminded us, are these: Sodom and Gomorrah, Nineveh and Tyre, Hiroshima and Nagasaki. And, as I speak, starvation's specter haunts Berlin and Calcutta. The death of the soul, creeping spiritual paralysis, has its fatal grip on the black-marketers and profiteers, who by their greed condemn others to death.

"All things work together for our good, if we love God." But we don't love God and if his mercy cannot reach us, then his warnings may.

Look at that *if*: there is no more important word for your soul than *if*. The Spartans were laconic people, brief in their replies. The story is old that King Philip of Macedonia, in his triumphant invading march met the Spartan leaders, and said "I will clear every woman and child out of your country if I enter Laconia." The Spartans looked at that menacing face, flushed with pride, and answered one word: "IF" What a mocking echo that was!

So, my people, is this if, a mocking monitor, to stab you awake, to get deep beneath that hard crust of self-satisfaction and to probe, like a spiritual surgeon, beneath the skin and flesh to the very heart of you?

Do you love God? Do you love God and serve him above all other masters; do you love him more than your own life? Or do you live with one eye on God and the other eye on the main chance? I am challenging youth in the morning of life; do you love God? I am challenging men and women here in the middle busy years of life; do you love God. I am challenging men and women in the evening of life; do you love God? I am preparing you all and myself before we stand in his presence, devoid of excuses beneath that searching glance of Holy Purity, because that is the question he will ask and he will know the answer.

He will know then how much of your time and thought was spent in the devout study of his Word at home and in the church. He will know whether you gave him of your heart's love ungrudgingly or whether you could not find ten minutes each morning and evening, or two hours on a Sunday to fill yourselves with his wisdom and his love. He will know whether you gave to his Son's church what was left over when you'd paid the bills of tradesman and the fees of pleasure or whether you did without some of these things for the love of God because they are more real. He will know whether you see yourself as superior to the common herd, and spoke uncharitably of those for whom Christ died, or whether you saw yourself as the undeserving servant of Christ, the Hope and Solace of the world. He will know whether you faced the disappointment of life, its hardships, its temptations, its bereavements, as messengers of God's trust in you and as trials of your faith, or whether you grumbled: "Why should this happen to me?" when the Crucifixion happened to your Lord.

I repeat, as the Gospel is always repeating from its Savior: Do you love God? "Son of Man, lovest Thou me?"

None of us, I hope, would cry in our heart of hearts: "Of course, Lord, you know that I love you." But, if we cannot say in sincerity "O Jesus Christ, my tortured and loving Savior, I am trying to love you more and more," our religion is a sham and our hope of happiness, and joy in this life and in the next is without foundation. We are building on nothing.

If we can say "I love God and I serve him and his church, and his children and I stake my life on that," then and then alone is this text a promise.

"All things work together for our good." Then we can say with St. Paul "I have learned in whatsoever state I am in therein to be content." For it is by the love of God alone that we can face up to life and find acceptance in it. That brilliant young novelist, Katherine Mansfield cried in the midst of her suffering: "O life, accept me, make me worthy, teach me." St. Paul knew the meaning of suffering was to make up what was lacking in the suffering of Christ. He was content.

And the realization that God was on his side made it possible to face anything, and everything. "If God be for us" he proclaims defiantly "who can be against us?" Then he ranges all the enemies of man in grim opposition, coming over the trenches to attack the Christian, as it were; together in bloodthirsty advance, crying vengeance with every desperate step, the bayonets flashing. Here they come: the torturer pain, the callous-eyed calamity, persecution, breathing hatred, the horrible skeleton of famine, penury and poverty ("nakedness," as he called it), danger, with the blood pouring from his eye-sockets, and the sword. He summons these hirelings of death to meet him in massed array. Into their very faces, he hurls the challenge and the assurance: "We Christians are conquerors. You shall not overcome. None of you shall divide us from the love of God in Christ."

We can face life like that because we know the worst in man, and we know the best in God. And our faith enables us to face up to life because God is for us.

"All things must work together for our good, if we love God." IF ...

I BELIEVE IN JESUS HIS ONLY SON OUR LORD

THE INCARNATION I

Is the Christmas story a lovely legend or is it eternal truth? Is it a pretty fable or is it historical fact?

I grant you that the whole thing sounds improbable, even impossible In the light of common day. It is daring, audaciously improbable. The Virgin visited by an angel; the birth of God in a stable because the inn was booked up, as if God could not have reserved rooms for this royal birth; the celestial singing that the shepherds heard and the bright star that the three kings followed. But the whole Gospel story is full of improbabilities. It is as difficult to believe that this helpless babe is Very God of Very God, as it is to believe that the Son of God worked until the perspiration damped his brow in a carpenter's shop; or that the outcast dispossessed on the cross was the Eternal Son of God. The whole thing is improbable.

And yet it was the only dignified way that God could have chosen to come into the world. A moment's thought will show you that Christ's coming was absolutely suitable to his divine mission. How right it was!

1. Suppose he had come in overwhelming power. Would you have had Christ come with the whole power of the universe behind him, using the stentorian voice that rolls the planets hurrying on their way? That was Jupiter's way, flinging thunderbolts from the blue. If God had chosen to cow men with his omnipotence, he would have been the bully of the universe. He would have used the same tactics as the big boy at school who twists the arm of the little, freckled boy in the lower form. The God who placed the shrinking, modest violet deep in the moss of the woods, who made the evening star to shine with subtle radiance in a crimson sky, who gave the tender love of men and women, could not be as vulgar as that. No, a demonstration of power would not be worthy of his graciousness.

2. Suppose he had come in infinite wisdom, a celestial school-teacher to scold the erring sons of men. Suppose he had overwhelmed us with his profundity, and silenced us with his cleverness. He would have been an intellectual prig. That would have been out of keeping with the character of God. Only small men parade their learning and air superior knowledge, as brutal

men parade their strength and rich men their wealth. The God we worship has better taste than that. He never spoke a word that wise men and shepherds would not hear together.

God comes to us in the only dignified way that he can. He comes in humility, taking on himself the form of a servant. He starts human life at scratch with us, possessing no privilege that leaves us out in the cold. He can say **Follow me** without any suggestion of absurdity. If a prize-fighter or a university professor or a millionaire were to say that, it would sound fantastically unreal. But Christ stands on common ground with us and has a right to say **Follow me.**

His humility was the only approach possible. That humility meant poverty. He was too poor to get into a full inn. A full inn? We've heard people say that before. It is amazing what a tip to the porter or the manager will do. That is the way of success as the world judges it. "I have influence. I know the manager." we say proudly. But Christ had no friends at court. He was too poor to find room in a full inn. He had to work for his living amidst the anxieties of a growing household. He had to remain at the carpenter's bench until full manhood, though he dreamed of a mission to save the world. He had to make ploughs and yokes until it seemed too late, for when he had his chance they put him to death.

He was too poor to buy his own grave. He would not openly advertise himself to be the son of God. "Not a word" he said, with his fingers on his lips. Someone asks in a crowded shop "Who is the Manager?" "I am," we say conscious of the deference due to our position. "If I am to be God, I must have the position due to my responsibilities." We cannot understand a God who does not want it to be known, a God who ministers without scepter in his hand, with only a towel and basin to wash the feet of the world.

He turns all our values topsy-turvy. If I had wanted to help the world I should have come as a ten-talent man scattering checks like autumn scattered leaves. But the difference with God is this. He shows us the Godlike things that we can do. He shows us not how to create worlds, but how to redeem them. That is something we can do. Not blasting enemies, but forgiving them; that we can do. Not sitting on a throne, but taking a towel and basin, articles that are found in the humblest home. God became man that we might become like God.

That is the God worshipped in our Christmas hymns and in our Communion: God in the cradle and in the shop, God on the cross.

What God bids us remember is that the Christmas story shows us not God in heaven, not God on the throne, but God on earth, God with us. If you want to be sure that God cares, this child in the manger, this young carpenter crucified felon among the thieves, these are the proofs that God hath visited and redeemed his people.

I close by quoting the great words of Kierkegaard: "Before trusting a man one asks him to give his word for it; thus God has given us his word for it: Christ is the Word."

And because of this trust the Christian is no longer an orphan in an unfriendly universe. When I look out from my window on a night starry like Bethlehem's greatest evening, I forget that those are scintillating fires in outer space; I can only think of them as the beckoning lights of home!

THE INCARNATION 2

> *"And in Jesus Christ his only Son our Lord,
> who was conceived by the Holy Ghost..."*

IS THE Christmas story a lovely legend? Or is it eternal truth? Is it a pretty fable or is it historical fact? Consider briefly the central article of the Apostles' Creed.

The supreme question that every Christian has to face is this: "What think you of Christ?" Is he a good man who was adopted by God as the Savior of the world? Or, is the Savior of the world, God the Son in the flesh? Do we worship a man who became God, or a God who became man?

The answer is we celebrate not the rising of a man to deity: but the infinite condescension of God to manhood. The Virgin Birth is simply a poetical and pictorial way of suggesting that the birth of Jesus was no ordinary birth. It was the fruit of divine initiative, with human co-operation, of the spirit of God and of Mary. The authority of Christ is not the authority of a human teacher, or of a prophet; it is the authority of the living God. The only-begotten Son alone knows the Father and has revealed him. The miracle of the Incarnation is not the Virgin-birth, but the miracle of God stooping to conquer. "Blessed be the Lord God of Israel because he hath visited and redeemed His people."

Halliday Sutherland has a story which illustrates the wonder and humility of the coming of God to earth. It is placed in the days when wagons and coaches were used instead of buses and motor-cars. The drivers of the older vehicles always had difficulties when they approached mountains. They had to ask the men and boys to step out of the coach and walk, just to lighten the load.

This made it easier for the horses to surmount the hills. On some occasions the gentlemen would refuse to give up their seats and neither flattery nor abuse would make them budge an inch. One famous driver had a never failing ruse that would cause the oldest gentlemen to dismount. He would say to them, as they approached the summit of the hill "Did you know that when the Prince of Wales was visiting the Highlands, he used to get out and walk at this point?" The words "Here the prince got out and walked" acted like magic. Even the oldest and feeblest would leap from their seats.

Now we have difficulties to face in our life. There are long hard roadways to walk along; there are steep hills to climb. Sometimes we long for someone to carry us over them or to be able to ride over them smoothly without discomfort. But we have a prince who got out and walked in Christ, the Prince of Life. He gave up his heavenly comfort to walk up the hills of Nazareth. He walks along three of the hardest roads:

1. The road of disappointment.

2. The road of suffering, paved with thorns.

3. The road of death that winds along the valley of the shadow.

It is that knowledge that God did not leave us alone but himself has walked along the hardest roads and up the highest hills, that gives us confidence. If the Prince got out and walked, then we have no right to ask for an easier way.

The Incarnation means that God understands, for he has walked this way before, with weary and lagging feet.

And when in your difficulties you cry out for help to Christ, it is not like appealing as a tramp in the limousine to the man in the limousine to understand, for he cannot. It is the cry of a wayfarer to life's pioneer. He knows the way. He IS the way.

Our greatest danger spiritually today is a willingness to be buddy with the Deity. We can call our equals comrades, but not our superior. No one who looked into the majestic eyes of the Christ could lightheartedly call him "Comrade." No one who had seen the hidden flashes of lightning of righteous indignation in his eyes, no one who had watched the infinite tenderness for the strugglers and the down-and-outs come into his eyes, like a great calm, could call this strange man equal.

Others abide our question. He is free. He questions us.

It is the poet Charles Lamb, not the theologians, who brings us nearest to the heart of the mystery of Christ's person. "There is only one other person" said Lamb, " . . . if Shakespeare were to come into the room, we should all rise to meet him. But if that Person were to come into it, we should all fall down and try to kiss the hem of His garment."

The last word is not argument: it is adoration in the presence of Christ. In him, God as man, we see the perfect revelation of God; in him we see the perfect man. The author of the Book of Revelation makes the true response.

The Incarnation 2

"And, when I saw him, I fell at His feet as one dead. And he laid his right hand upon me, saying: 'Fear not, I am the first and the last and the living one; and I was dead and behold, I am alive for evermore, and I have the keys of death and of Hades.'"

He is the Lord of Life and of Death, the King of King and Lord of Lords, who by his suffering has brought peace to our souls, by his teaching sanity, and by his Resurrection, brought us into a heritage that overleaps the obstacles of life.

THE DIVINITY OF OUR LORD I

CONSIDER TWO clues to the mystery of Our Lord's Person:

(1) That he could only be a true example and guide to us if he had undergone human suffering and human temptations. He must be truly human, a man, to be our elder brother.

(2) At the same time, he must be divine: for he must speak to us in the name and with the authority or God. Only God can redeem us. And it is this belief that Jesus was the Divine Son of God who came to earth for us that the great creeds enshrine.

But now tonight, let us to leave these theological thoughts in the background. Instead, let us simply look through the Gospels to see "What manner of man is this?"

I. His External Appearance

1. Jesus must have been unmistakably attractive. This we can gather by the tribute of the woman who said on the Jerusalem roadside: "Blessed is the womb that bore Thee and the breasts which thou didst suck." That is simply a Hebrew mode of saying: "I wish he had been my Son, this handsome figure of a man."

2. Quite obviously, too, Jesus must have had striking eyes. St. Mark is always drawing attention to them. "And when he had looked round about on them with anger" what lightning of displeasure flashed in those magnificent eyes. Then the rich young ruler also speaks of them: "And Jesus looking upon him loved him." Now the eyes have a blue lambent flame of lingering tenderness. He himself says once: "the light of thy body is thine eye. If thine eye be single, thy whole body shall be full of light." What light shone forth from his eyes!

3. We get beside this exterior comeliness an impression of energy, vigor and health. Here Jesus is a complete contrast to Mohammed who was a sickly man, wasting under a hereditary disease. He also is in complete contrast to Buddha who was mentally and nervously broken down when he died.

We notice that Jesus arose with the dawn or before it, as noted in Mark 1:35. "And in the morning, a great while before day, he rose up, and went out, and departed into a desert place, and there prayed." We see also that he was a lover of nature. He was familiar with the hills, the lakes and the valleys and loved to wander there. That he was physically in splendid health is proved by the wearisome journeys he made through mountainous country with the simplest of provisions and he expects the same of his disciples. "And he said unto them: Take nothing for your journey, neither staff, nor wallet, nor bread, nor money; neither have two coats."

Other proof, if any were needed of his robustness, is the last journey he took from Jericho to Jerusalem. This was an astonishing feat. He climbed a height of 3,500 feet in six hours and was so unwearied that the same evening he joined in the feast that Lazarus and his two sisters had prepared in Bethany a few miles out of Jerusalem.

Then again this man had no home or house. He lived a hardy life, a Spartan existence. The only houses he entered belonged to friends or acquaintances "Birds have nests"; he said "foxes have-holes; but the Son of man hath not where to lay his head." Take it at its face value and it means that Jesus must have spent night after night out in the open.

Then notice how unreservedly he gave himself to his work and how exhausting that must have been. On two occasions St. Mark notes that he had so much work to do that he had not time even to snatch a hurried meal (Mark 3:28 and 6:31.) "For there were many coming and going and they had not leisure so much as to eat." Often they worked until late in the evening healing the lame, exorcising evil spirits, giving counsel to those in trouble. He did this as well as confuting the Pharisees and Sadducees in public argument. Add to all this the time he spent in answering the questions of the disciples and training them for their apostleship.

Here then was a handsome figure, with fascinating eyes, an immense love for the open-air life, a robust constitution, working with superhuman zest in healing, teaching, reproving, confuting and advising. But what of his mental powers?

II. His Mental Powers

It has been suggested that he was unbalanced, a visionary or a fanatic, and that the first suspicions of his family were justified. What impression do his mental powers make upon us?

    a. The first thing we notice is that he is not given to moods like the visionary. He does not, like the fanatic, have bees in his bonnet, strange and

The Divinity of our Lord 1

fantastic notions. On the contrary, we are impressed by his remarkable fixity of purpose, his definite, undeviating aims. There is nothing vague or sentimental or contradictory about Jesus.

You see it in the finality of his very phrases. "I am God's shepherd ... I came not to call the righteous but sinners." Or "The Son of man came not to be ministered to, but to minister and to give his life a ransom for many." He is terse, compact; there is no possibility of misunderstanding him.

He knew his mission. Even as a twelve-year child in the Temple: "I must be about my Father's business." He saw through the subtle temptations to minister to his vanity in the wilderness and finally put them on one side as undesirable. Sometimes his disciples were opposed to his plans, but he was inflexible. When Peter tried to dissuade him from trading the *via dolorosa* to the Cross, Jesus said "Get thee behind me Satan." He advised his disciples: "Let your speech be Yea, Yea; Nay, Nay." His own speech was as definite.

b. Notice how he takes the heroic, austere life for granted. The rich young ruler is expected, without hesitation, to sell all his possessions and give them to the poor, and then to follow him. Another time, he says that family occasions must not deter a man from following him immediately. "Let the dead bury their own dead." For him the heroic life was the natural life.

c. Notice how his resolution made him a born leader. He gave orders; instantly he was obeyed. He beckons Andrew and Simon to follow him from their boats. "Immediately, leaving their nets, they followed Him." The disciples were awed by him and the multitude knew he was a man of supreme authority. It was said on all hands "that He speaketh with authority and not like the scribes."

d. Another facet of his character is his stern reproof of evil. He says to the devil "Be gone, Satan." He calls the Pharisees "You whited sepulchers"; to the money changers, he speaks in no uncertain terms: "You have changed my Father's house into a den of thieves." He is, we see, resolute, commanding, majestic, fearless, and certain of his mission to the world, a leader.

The question now arises: was Jesus anything more than a radical, a prophet who wished to sweep away the entire old world and inaugurate a new one? Was he a mystic, a visionary?

He was not. Mohammed had trances and visions; so did St. Paul, but not Jesus. Look at his eminently practical qualities.

1. He was excellent in subtle argument: a) against the Saducees who asked him to give a sign from heaven, and b) against the Pharisees who asked him about divorce and paying tax: "Render unto Caesar what belongs to Caesar and to God what belongs to God." He had a clear and a sharp brain.

2. His ability to delve down to the motives of men was also remarkable: "Let him who is without sin cast the first stone." He did not follow ritual observance but had the humility of the child-mind.

3. He had immense power of detailed observation of Palestinian life as expressed in parables. He showed the life of fisher folks, peasants, merchants, vintners, builders, children in streets, rich farmers hugging barns, and a woman who lost a coin. He evoked wedding processions, ceremonial precedence at wealthy dinners etc.

III. Jesus as a Realist

Jesus was a realist. He has no vague dreams about a regenerate humanity.

1. He recognizes the diabolical power of evil. He names: "This wicked and adulterous generation." Or he speaks of "Galileans whose blood mingled with their sacrifices" etc.

2. He knows our human frailty. "Judge not that ye be not judged." "Why beholdest thou the mote that is in thy brother's eye, but not beam in thy own?" He was under no illusions.

3. He does not theorize about difficulties, but offers practical sympathy and compassion. He has a decided preference for the poor and the needy because they are more ready to receive gospel, and they need his friendship. We notice he is not oblivious of human need. He is not otherworldly. He lives with the publicans and sinners. He understands and listens. He does not condemn from the outside. He shares.

4. He did not shun human joys and pleasures. There again he appears marvelously balanced. He was called a glutton and a winebibber. He shows sheer enjoyment of nature and of human fellowship, as in the miracle at the Cana wedding.

Can we sum up? He was comely, with flashing eyes, a robust personality and immense resources of energy, an untiring worker.

Mentally, he was clear, concise, and definite. Majestic and commanding, he proved to be a born leader, fearless in denouncing evil. The heroic life was commonplace for him. He was exceedingly subtle in argument, penetrating in his insight into human motives, gifted with a great power of observing details.

He was the complete realist. He knew the sheer evil in the life of men. His help was not words or theory, but practical compassion, sharing the life of the needy, living amongst them, and loving them to improvement. Yet strict as he was in his desire to inaugurate the Kingdom, he was no John the Baptist shunning the joys of humankind. He loved fellowship and was a guest as the wedding feast in Cana.

Such is the vivid personality of Our Lord. It is a straight-cut diamond, obviously genuine, through and through consistently heroic.

And yet he combines in his character qualities that, singly found, are remarkable in men, but together have never before or since been combined in one towering personality. His life has two tendencies: an upward thrust in utter devotion to God, his beloved Father, and a downward leaning towards outgoing service to men and women.

In conclusion, I ask you simply to note the amazing qualities that are found perfectly balanced in his nature.

Regal and majestic, yet he washes the feet of his disciples.

Impetuous and harsh to hypocrites, he is yet tender to the repentant and the wronged as a mother.

Wholly hallowed to God by nights of prayer, yet he foregathers with publicans and sinners.

Dedicated to the infinite and celestial, yet his eye sees the beauty of the meanest flower.

Prophetic firebrand blazing in wrath, yet in his own person he submits to the foulest iniquities in silence.

Uniquely solitary, yet he loves men and dies for love of them.

Who is this Jesus? Already we can say: "Never was man like this man!" This is only a hairbreadth from Thomas's confession "My Lord and my God."

THE DIVINITY OF OUR LORD 2

LET US examine the prayer-life of Jesus, to see if we can discover what was different in him from other men. Our aim will be to find out what spiritual aims dominated and animated him.

I. His Prayer

That can be answered immediately: the main spring of his actions was complete surrender to his Father's will. It was nothing less than a burning and blazing love for his heavenly Father. His life was a perfect sermon on the text "Thou shalt love the Lord with thy whole heart and thy whole soul and with thy whole strength." (Deut. 6:5.) The first recorded words of our Lord are a reminder that his home is with the Father: "Did you not know that I must be about my Father's business?" and his last dying words are breathed in the ear of his Father: "Father into Thy hands I commend my spirit."

Again and again the evangelists record his profound intimacy with God the Father. When he was baptized, Jesus prayed and "heaven was opened." When he decided to choose his disciples: "He went out into a mountain to pray and he passed the whole night in the prayer to God." And when the day was come, he called unto him his disciples. (Luke 6:12–13) Most of his actions were the fruit of his prayer life; for instance the healing of the deaf-mute, the healing of the boy possessed by the dumb-spirit, the raising of Lazarus from the dead and the multiplication of the loaves. When the disciples returned from their successful mission, he rejoiced in the Holy Ghost and said "I confess to Thee, O Father, Lord of Heaven and earth."

The whole of his Passion breathes the Spirit of nobility and prayer. In the Upper Room he dedicates himself and his followers, and institutes with thanksgiving and benediction the new covenant in his blood. In Gethsemane "He fell upon His face praying and saying: 'Father, if it be possible let this cup pass away from me.'" And his agonizing death upon Golgotha was like a struggle to do the will of his Father, maintained by ever new supplication to him.

From this account of the life of Jesus we see plainly that the golden background to all his words and works was his intimate sense of union with God the Father. It is the very oxygen of his soul, the breath of his spiritual life. God was powerful; God was holy; God was loving.

II. His Prayers

As we watch Jesus praying, we see that Jesus is wholly himself when he is alone with God. What are the outstanding features of his prayer-life?

1. Notice the modesty and seclusion in which it is made. When he exhorts his disciples: "When thou shalt pray, enter into thy chamber, and having shut the door, pray to thy Father in secret," he is telling them to follow his own practice. There is no place he likes better to pray in than solitude. "And having dismissed the multitude, He went into a mountain alone to pray." In the loneliness of the night, when even the sun rays and the grasses of the field are sleeping, was when he found his Father and was alone with him. He felt most himself when alone with God.

2. Notice the directness of his prayers. They are the result of a living experience with God, unlike the prayers of St. Paul, they are simple and homely, short and to the point, like little arrow prayers. "Father I give Thee thanks that Thou hast heard me." (John 11:41) "Father, not as I will; but as Thou wilt." (Matthew 26:29.) "Thou hast hid these things from the wise and prudent and hast revealed them to little ones. Yea, Father, for so it hath seemed good in Thy sight." Nothing could be simpler, warmer, and more intimate.

3. A strange mystery, notice that Jesus never makes a confession of sin to God. When a man or even a saint prays, his prayer is always a cry from the depths of human frailty and moral guilt, a prayer of awe in the face of the absolute holiness of God. It is essentially a "Lord have mercy upon me." In fact, usually the purer a Christian strives to make his life, the more plainly and terrifying does he see the immense hollowness and hypocrisy of his life when viewed in the Divine light. It is entirely different in the case of Jesus. The only time he utters "Forgive us our trespasses and deliver us from evil." Is when he is providing a pattern of prayer for his disciples to use? Never did he use this petition personally. The cry, "Father, forgive Me." never passes his lips. Even when the terrors of death surrounded him and a sense of utter dereliction weighed down his soul, no one heard him cry thus. They only heard the cry "Father, forgive them."

He prays as one who does not know sin. That is why petitions are so rare a part of his .prayers, and why we nearly always hear acts of praise and thanksgiving, an exultant outpouring of grateful joy to the Father. "Father, I give Thee thanks" is his usual prayer.

Then again, when he does pray for something, it is not a worried, anxious petition, but a confident request, certain that it will be granted. It is like an appeal to his native right, as in the prayer "Father, I will that where I am, there also those whom thou hast given me, may be also." (John 17:24.)

The fact is that Jesus does not stand before his heavenly Father as a beggar, still less as a prodigal son. He looks up at him with the untroubled, glowing eyes of a child. As if it were the most natural thing in the world, he unites himself with him in the most familiar and intimate personal communion. Never, since prayer and sacrifice were offered up on earth, has anyone, be he sinner or saint, thus prayed.

When we realize this, we can only come to one conclusion: "He was tempted at all points as we are, yet without sin." That is the verdict of the Epistle to the Hebrews. It must be your verdict and mine, as we have looked at the prayer-life of the Christ of God.

III. Courage and Confidence

We shall not be long in discovering that the incomparable courage of Jesus springs out of his absolute trust in the Father. Jesus rarely wonders: "Where is your faith?" he asks of his disciples in the midst of the tempest. "Fear not; only believe" is what he says to a father, standing before the dead body of his child. Even the most dreadful things that can befall a father are for Jesus no cause for fear or concern. Anxiety is something absolutely alien and foreign to Jesus.

He is under no delusion about the dangers that threaten his followers: "Behold, I send you as sheep in the midst of wolves." But stronger than any danger is his absolute confidence in the Father. "Be not solicitous, therefore, saying: What shall we eat or what shall we drink, or wherewithal shall we be clothed? For after these things do the heathens seek? For your Father knoweth that ye have need of these things."

We are at the limit of understanding and can go no further. Who is this Jesus who can pray so holily, who lives so confidently and dies so guiltlessly? There is in him a holy folly, an excess of faith and trust, a lavishness of moral strength, incredible purity and tenderness. His life is a festival of God. When has there ever appeared on earth a being like unto him? All human standards fail us here. The religious, intellectual and moral stature of Jesus reaches dimensions beyond any measurement. His life is like a rare poem from a foreign land, and yet it is a living reality. What is told of him is all unpremeditated, inimitable, uninventable. It is so graven into his concrete, work-a-day life that we stand on the bedrock of history. Once upon a time there was actually a man who knew himself to be in the most intimate union of life and love with his father in Heaven, who saw God's creative power at work as if with the naked eye, and whose appearance on the scene of history was an apparition of sanctity.

Who was this man Jesus? We shall be able to answer the question more fully when we think of Christ's self-revelation of his personal purpose but surely we must say: this is the eternal Son of God, who in his life shows us the nature of God, and the nature of man as God meant it to be. We can guess his secret from his own words: "I was before Abraham," and elsewhere "I and the Father are one." He was the eternal son of God in the flesh, very God and very man.

THE DIVINITY OF OUR LORD 3

The Son of Man

WHAT HAS Jesus to tell us of himself? Let us analyze the title "Son of Man." That will take us a long way into the mystery of Christ's person. What did Jesus mean by this title? Ever since Daniel 7:13. had spoken of one "Who like the Son of man came with clouds of heaven," the title implied the coming Messiah who would, at the end of time, redeem Israel.

It was not as clear or definite a title as the term "Son of God." The term had a strange undertone. "Son of God" inevitably made people think of a great King of the line of David who should restore Israel to national and commercial prosperity. If he had used this term it would have obscured his secret—and people would have expected a military general or a national, instead of a spiritual leader.

If he had taken to himself the name of Yahweh—God—his countrymen would have stoned him for blasphemy at the very outset of his career.

So he took this mysterious term "The Son of Man" because it made men think of supernatural, divine spheres, the right hand of the Ancient of days. Whenever Jesus speaks of the last day of time, he speaks of the Son of Man sitting on the right hand of the power of God and coming with the clouds of Heaven. "And then shall they see the Son of Man coming in clouds with great glory and power. And then shall he send forth the angels and shall gather together his elect from the four winds . . ." (Mark 13:26–27) With absolute assurance of his mission, he knows from the outset that this prophecy is fulfilled in his person. In Daniel's picture of the Son of Man, he reveals himself as the Judge of the World and as the Lord of the new kingdom descending from heaven. He is Lord now and shall be Lord on the Day of Judgment.

This, the claim of Jesus to be Son of Man runs parallel with St. John's phrase "The Word became flesh." We have in him an appearance of the divine in the garb of the human. Our attitude to his person in time is decisive for all eternally. Therefore he can say: "Every one that shall confess me before men,

I will also confess him before my Father which is in heaven. But he that shall deny me before men, I will also deny him before my Father who is in heaven." (Matthew 10:32 . . .)

But this phrase "The Son of Man" refers in Daniel only to the last judgment. Our Lord uses the term to apply to himself in the present tense. He is present Savior as well as future Judge. He says "Blessed are the eyes that see the things you see. For I say unto you that many prophets and kings have desired to see the things that you see and have not seen them." Jesus is in fact the present King of the Kingdom of God. "Come unto me all ye that labor and are heavy laden and I will give you refreshment." He is the present Redeemer, "The Son of Man is come to seek and to save that which is lost." (Luke 19:10.)

Jesus is able to change the laws of God. Even so venerable a law as the Sabbath is altered by him. "The Son of Man is Lord of the Sabbath."

Furthermore he does what God alone can do. He forgives sins and says he does so "That you may know the Son of Man hath power on earth to forgive sins," He sayeth to the sick of the palsy, "I say to thee: Arise, take up thy bed, and go into thy house." (Mark 2:48.) There is the same claim in his words to the sinful woman "Thy sins are forgiven thee." (Luke 7:48.) Here Jesus is not merely at the right hand of God; he has attained to his heart.

Then, again, the Son of Man must win his Redeemership over the souls of men by his Passion. He will be the Redeemer of men only when he has shed his life's blood for them. Again and again he predicts the Cross by saying: "The Son of Man must suffer." (Mark 8:31, 9:12; Matthew 16:21; Luke 9:22.). "The Son of Man is not come to be ministered to, but to minister and to give his life as ransom for many."

In this little phrase "the Son of Man" are concealed the most tremendous contrasts in the consciousness he had of himself. Jesus knows himself to be exalted to the heavens; and he also sees himself thrown down into the slime of the earth. He is come to rule; he is also come to minister and die. King of the kingdom, he is, and also the slave of men. We can now understand why Jesus took by preference the name Son of Man—so that by its simple symbolism he might show what he intends to be for man, a man among men and yet their King and judge, and their Savior: a man from heaven.

We now reach the supreme question: was Jesus a creature of God, or God himself in the flesh? Is he distinct from God or one with God? What is his position in the scale of beings?

I. To begin with he was infinitely superior to all the prophets. John the Baptist is greater than all that are born of women, greater, that is, than all the

The Divinity of Our Lord 3

prophets and kings of the Old Covenant, and yet he confesses that "he that is least in the kingdom of heaven is greater than he." (Matthew 11:11.) Jesus is conscious that their work is preparation, his consummation and fulfillment. When for the first time he revisits Nazareth, he says: "this day is fulfilled the Scripture of Isaiah which proclaims healing to the poor, deliverance to the oppressed and captives, and sight to the blind."

He has a boundless authority in his own person. The greatest thing in the old Covenant was the Temple—but even that was subject to his authority. "I tell you that there is here a greater than the Temple." (Matthew 12:6.) The all holy God gave the law through his servant Moses, but Jesus goes beyond Moses and in the name of a new inwardness and love. "The Son of Man is Lord of the Sabbath." He corrects the precepts of Moses no less than six times. He does not claim the special revelation of a prophet, nor say, as they did, "Thus saith the Lord." He says simply, "But I say unto you . . . ." He claims the authority of God himself.

We see the same authority in the miracles. These are not answers to prayer, but the simple operations of his own being. It is not from the Father but from himself the influence proceeds. He says: "I will. Be thou made clean." (to the leper). "Ephphatha . . . be thou opened!" (to the deaf man). "Talitha cumi . . . Damsel, I say unto thee, arise." (to the daughter of the ruler of the synagogue). "Arise, take up thy bed and go into thy house." (to the man sick of the palsy). Here is not a divine commission, or delegated power. This is omnipotence in the flesh.

If we needed more evidence that Jesus identified himself with God, we should find it in descriptions of himself.

He was the wonder-working God foretold by Isaiah. "And Jesus answered and said unto them: Go and tell John the things ye see and hear the blind receive their sight, and the lame walk, lepers are cleansed, and the deaf near, and the dead are raised up, and the poor have good tidings preached unto them, (Matthew 11:5).

He is himself the Good Shepherd whom Isaiah (40) and Ezekiel (34) look for as God to be. As Jehovah is described by Jeremiah and Ezekiel as the husband of Israel, he calls himself the bridegroom of his followers.

Need we look any further? The origin of this new and incomparably pure and holy humanity is God himself. It is only because Jesus is God that the human character of Jesus is a manifestation of the divine.

It is this alone that explains why his teaching embraces the present and the future, the new kingdom and the future judgment.

It is this alone that explains why Jesus makes his person the centre of his teaching. Jesus did not demand attachment to his teaching, as did Buddha or Mohammed; he demanded attachment to himself. "You believe in God, believe also in me.... He that loveth father and mother more than me is not worthy of me." Jesus is not merely with God. He is God himself.

St. John saw it clearly, beholding the glory of God in his face: "the glory as it were, of the only-begotten of the Father." It was this impression of sheer Deity that made the man with the unclean spirit cry out: "Thou art the Holy One of God." It brought the confession from the centurion: "I am not worthy that thou shouldst enter under my roof." It brought Peter to his knees: "Depart from me, for I am a sinful man, O Lord." It was this that Jesus declared himself when he said: "No one knoweth who the Son is but the Father; and who the Father is but the Son." Thus God the Father stands in unique relationship with God the Son. "He that hath seen me hath seen the Father." The veil over the mystery of his personality falls away as Jesus opens his heart to God in the prayer of the Upper Room: "Holy Father the world has not known Thee: but I have known and these have known that Thou hast sent me." Dare we refuse to acknowledge him as God who said: "I and the Father are one?"

This is the glory of the Christian religion: the wonder that the eternal Son of God emptied himself of his divine majesty, to become the servant of men, as a man.

Must we not bow with Chesterton in reverent astonishment at the condescension of Christ? Must we not as Chesterton says, expect the grass to wither and the birds to drop dead out of the air, when a strolling carpenter's apprentice says calmly and almost carelessly: "Before Abraham was I am" and "I and the Father are one."

And God himself gave his approval to our judgment, that this is the everlasting Son of the Father in the flesh. That is the meaning of the Resurrection. Unmistakably, for the entire world to see, God declares: "This is my beloved Son in whom I am well pleased."

We cannot go deeper than the Ancient Creeds. For the right faith is that we believe and confess that our Lord Jesus Christ the Son of God is God and man. He is God of the substance of the Father, begotten before the world; and he is man of the substance of his mother, born in the world. He is perfect God and perfect man.

"I believe in God the Father Almighty ... and in Jesus Christ his only Son our Lord ... I believe in the Holy Ghost...." (The Apostles' Creed.)

GOD'S COVENANT WITH MEN

Jesus the mediator of a new Covenant.
—Hebrews 12:24

I wonder how many of you could define the word covenant and describe what a covenant is? It is one of our great biblical words which has gone out of fashion. I suppose that if you were to look for a modern word to take its place, the best would be contract or agreement.

But these words are very poor substitutes for covenant because the old word is hallowed by religious usage and the newer equivalents are a little soiled with business and prudential considerations. To talk of contract between God and Man—a quid pro quo—is to reduce the operations of the grace of God and the voluntary response of man to the levels of bargain. This will not do.

I. What Is a Covenant?

Before you can understand the meaning of covenant, you ought to see an ancient covenant. Last summer in the Bodleian Library in Oxford, there was an exhibition of them. These covenants dated from Edward the Confessor's time to Queen Victoria's. The earliest of them were written in a flourishing hand on mellow parchment and, when completed, they were tied together with red ribbon. Many of them were agreements between the Kings of England and their subjects, in which the King granted a piece of land to a subject for a long lease in return for the production of so many men to fight in the King's army. The authenticity of them was guaranteed by an elaborate seal with the royal coat of arms. They were more personal than the modern type-written documents and more dignified. They showed quite clearly that a covenant was a solemn agreement entered into by two parties: one the King and the other, the subject, signed and sealed. And this is exactly what a religious covenant was: an agreement between the King of the Universe and his subjects, signed and sealed.

The first great covenant of the Bible was granted at Mount Sinai. There the conditions of the agreement were the Ten Commandments, if the children of Israel would obey them, then God would be their God, and they would be his people.

But this was broken; such is the faithlessness of human nature. And centuries later, Jeremiah looked forward to a new agreement between God and his people, in which the bond of union would be a natural love of God, not a desire for reciprocal advantages as the old one was. This expectation was fulfilled, in Jesus: "Jesus the new Mediator of a new Covenant." If we may use the language of an older day, the covenant was ratified with his blood. His mark was the Cross and the seal was his life-blood.

In our modern emphasis upon the teaching of Jesus, let us not forget the importance of the person of Jesus. What he was is even more important than what he said. And one of the things that he said gives us a clue to his importance: "No man comes to the Father but by me." He was the Sole Mediator. "There is no other name under Heaven whereby we must be saved." Exclusive claims indeed, but his position was unparalleled. It means nothing less than it says: He is the only way to the Father; he is the only way to eternal life.

II. What Is the Covenant That He Brings?

There are two parties to every agreement. Here the first is God; the second is man. God offers man three essential things:

1. He grants the power to produce the best in man: so that he shall not be perpetually disgracing himself by meanness, pettiness, introspection, greed... Indeed he releases from all the indignities of human nature that we label under the one ugly heading of sin.

2. He offers him a full and free pardon for all his past misdemeanors. For one who had expected such high things from men and received such disappointing and insulting results, it is not an easy thing to give. But the gift gives the torn conscience balm and ease of mind.

3. Thirdly, he offers an utterly new quality of life here and now, and in the world to come: a kind of life in which man will be able to face every earthly disappointment and bereavement with resolution and radiance, where despair is impossible and man achieves a detachment, living on the hill-tops of life even when he is in the smoke-begrimed towns. He may be dirtied by life, but never defeated by it. These inestimable gifts then are offered: power, pardon and peace.

III. What Does God Require?

What does God require in return? He requires a whole-hearted obedience to Christ and his church. To refuse them is to refuse God's gifts. What does this mean when translated into practical terms? I think it means three things. It means Creed, Conduct and Comradeliness.

1. First it means Creed. A man is a Christian primarily because he believes in Christ. And his belief must be more than a sentimental attitude towards a Savior. The advice of I Peter 3:15–16 is still necessary: "Sanctify in your hearts Christ as Lord; being always ready to give answer to every man that asketh you a reason for the hope that is in you." A man who does not know why he is a Christian is not a Christian. And a man is a Christian only because he knows of the mighty acts of God effected in Jesus Christ. He must therefore be able to make some such statement as this:

> We believe in Thee, O God: the Father Almighty, Maker of all things visible and invisible; Thou art God eternal: heaven and earth are full of the majesty of Thy glory.
>
> We believe in Jesus Christ, Thy unique Son: the true light that lighteth every man; the express image of thy goodness; who for us men and our salvation, lived in this world, and died upon the cross: yet behold, He is alive for evermore, our Lord and Judge.
>
> We believe in the Holy Spirit, giver of life and grace, who sheweth us Thy way of freedom, truth and love.
>
> We believe in the Universal church, Christ's fellowship in earth and heaven: the Communion of saints; the Forgiveness of sins; and Life in Thee, which shall have no end.

In other words a Christian man must believe that God is Creator, that Christ is Redeemer, that the Holy Spirit is Inspirer; he must accept the Incarnation and the Resurrection and believe in the forgiveness of sins and eternal life. It is not sufficient to say: "I love Jesus Christ."

Secondly, such a vigorous creed demands conduct that will defend it and uphold it. I Peter again insists: "Have a good conscience; that wherein ye are spoken against, they may be put to shame who revile your good manner of life in Christ."

Thirdly, and I want to dwell at length on this, acceptance of Christ means acceptance of his church. You cannot have Christianity without the church. Even groups or organizations, who claim to be superior to the church, and to live the Christian life outside it, are very inconsistent in this. For if the church had not preserved the Bible, and taught it through the centuries, Christianity would no longer exist.

I Believe in Jesus His Only Son Our Lord

I heartily endorse the words of John Calvin: "He cannot have God as His Father who has not the Church as his Mother." And let me quote words written by the headmaster of Rugby in a recent volume entitled *Towards a Christian Order*. Hugh Lyon writes:

> Christianity never was and never could have been a purely personal religion: it was from the first the faith of a community. And it is on the expression of this faith in communal worship that its strength has always rested. Persecution has never driven Christians apart from one another; whether in Roman catacombs, on Scottish hillsides or in German cellars. They have always come secretly together, forced by their adversity to affirm still more strongly their need to worship, and strengthened by that worship to endure.

If you are really engaged to be the Lord's, the strongest possible obligation rests upon you to attend worship regularly. And it is a very paltry pretence you make at being a Christian if a warm bed or a cold morning decides whether you shall worship God.

How do you think Christianity has a hope of conquering the world with half empty churches? People judge the power of organizations by the enthusiasm and numbers of its supporters. A stranger entering our church might think that we were the lingering remnants of an outworn superstition, rather than the armies of the living God. So that as a testimony of your sincerity to God, make regular worship your concern, now. And if you come at personal inconvenience and when you are not in the mood, you bring a greater tribute to God. But how can we hope to conquer the world, if Christ does not appear to have defeated your lassitude?

In the second place, you will attend the Lord's Supper diligently. Our forefathers called this the seal of the seal of the Covenant. They meant that God brings home his promises to us in the intimate fellowship around Christ's table, and to keep that honorably is the only important resolution for us this year. No man with a spark of spiritual sensitivity left in him can fail to be kindled to new enthusiasm by the dying commands of Jesus Christ. No man can eat at his holy table without a sincere confession of sin; no man can rise from that table without avowing to live a more honorable life. No man returns to the hurly-burly of life without a deeper sense of knowing the ultimate mystery and meaning of life. Neglect this ordinance only at the cost of allowing the conscience to degenerate and the spiritual enthusiasm to evaporate.

Thirdly, an obedience to Christ demands that you no longer sit loose to the fellowship of the church. You are a poor, timid follower of the Savior if you will not contract yourself to him by the vows of church membership. Are you disappointed in the church? Then all the more reason why you should join. We need your help. And it is only within the fellowship of Christ's members that you can meet with man and women of every walk of life with complete ease and without affectation. It is the truest democracy: in the presence of Christ we are all equals. Over the door of the original Toch H at Popperinghe were the words: "Abandon rank, all ye who enter here." And I believe it would not be wrong to make this claim for our own church, here.

I shall say little about giving for the cause of Christ. It might look as if I were begging for my own salary. But this I will say; in the much maligned Victorian days it was not uncommon for business men to put aside ten per cent of their income for church contributions; anything over and above that was called a Free-will offering. Conditions are different today. But I hope the cause of Christ costs you at least as much as you spend on amusements. If it doesn't, you are only playing at being a Christian. Remember that you have entered into a solemn covenant with God.

THE ATONEMENT: DIVINE BLOOD-TRANSFUSION

"He suffered under Pontius Pilate, was crucified, dead, and buried ... and ... I believe ... in the forgiveness of sins."

PROFESSOR WILLIAM James in his great book *The Varieties of Religious Experience* studied all the great religions of the world. He found that they all had two convictions in common: first "a sense that there is something wrong about us as we naturally stand" and secondly "a sense that we are saved from this wrongness by making proper connection with the higher powers."

We are religious only because we have a sense of sin. This is the history of religion. David cries: "Against Thee, Thee only have I sinned." Peter cries: "Depart from me, O Lord, for I am a sinful man." St. Paul laments: "The evil that I would not that I do." Luther beseeches: "Out of the depths, I cry to Thee ..." The most ancient liturgies of the East and the West repeat the threefold entreaty: "Lord have mercy upon us. Christ have mercy upon us, Lord have mercy upon us." The General Confession echoes the same strains: "We have erred and strayed from thy ways like lost sheep. We have followed too much the devices and desires of our own hearts. We have offended against thy holy laws." And only a few years ago G.K. Chesterton gave his reason for entering the Roman Church in six simple words: "To get rid of my sins."

All altars with their pathetic sacrifices to allay the terrors of God, all his temples and churches where he might consult the sacred oracle and all his churches are the monuments of an everlastingly guilty conscience. All of them cry in stone: "Lord, have mercy on us."

Religion is begotten in despair. The death of pride is the birth of faith. Religion is man's desperate S.O.S.

And the answer of God to the piteous cry of our humanity is seen in its totality on the Cross of Calvary. You will all have heard the stirring Negro spiritual which chants: "Were you there when they crucified my Lord?" The answer of the Christian must be "Yes," because he is such a one as crucifies Christ afresh. The Cross is not simply an event in history; it is an event in our spiritual experience. The sinner recognizes himself in his true colors before the baleful light of the ghastly tree. That is the first meaning of salvation: we see in the Cross of Christ, the absolute foulness and cruelty and absurdity of sin. If you have not been there when they crucified your Lord, you are not even on the road to recovery. You have not learned the plight you are in. But if you have watched the most staggering injustice in history, then you know the diabolical element that wars in every one of us.

Look carefully at the accomplices of the crime. There is silent, cynical, irresponsible Pilate who believes that Jesus is speaking the truth but washes his hands of responsibility. There is the appeaser, the man who sells justice to the Jewish leaders. There "Peace at any price" is nakedly exposed. Watch the Pharisees, the Sadducees, and the Zealots. They had only one aim: to silence opposition to their own views, to claim their own privileges. They crushed the opposition by killing it. They wanted the Messiah to be their mouthpiece and not the mouth of the ever living God.

Watch the disciples. Watch Judas, whom Dante put in the lowest cauldron of Hell; see there the ghastliness of greed. Watch Peter, the Peter who was going to die for Christ, ashamed to confess his Lord to a servant-girl. And look at the rest of his friends, a pack of cowards, skulking behind a barricaded room in Jerusalem. And watch the crowd, fickle, unreliable; they who wanted to crown him now want to crucify him.

Picture the scene in all its tragic irony. He is the perfect Son of God transfixed between a couple of common thieves, with Roman soldiers dicing at his feet for his clothes.

We know that he should still be walking the valleys and the hills of Palestine curing and comforting, helping and healing. And on the hill of Calvary, there should have been a Cross for every one who conspired in the greatest crime against God's holiness. They should be writhing in agony and he should be free. And through the foulness and horror of human sin, the situation is reversed. The Messiah is murdered and the murderers go scot free.

There in one grim scene is shown the absolute horror of sin. When God comes to show us eternal life, we kill him. Oh, the disappointment of God and the ingratitude of man!

But if this scene is a revelation of man's utter and complete defeat, it is also a revelation of God's reconciliation. It shows not only the horror of sin, but the moans of defeating sin. In that, cross is our salvation.

Now if there is one phrase which we moderns avoid, it is this: saved by the blood of the Lamb. And it is precisely this old evangelical phrase, when properly understood, that describes the truth of our salvation; the inner

The Atonement: Divine Blood-Transfusion

meaning of the Cross from God's side. We are saved by the blood of Christ, but how? We are saved by the perfect self-offering of Christ on the Cross.

(1). There are three ways in which The Sacrifice of Christ reconciles us to God. In the first place, the self-offering of Jesus is his perfect obedience to the Father's will. He alone offers to his Divine Father the obedience which men ought to offer to God, and which they would offer if they fulfilled the obligations of sonship. In the Cross Christ represents men through his obedience in suffering. He does it in their names and for their sakes. Men are rebels, but because of the loyalty of Christ, God accepts them, when they unite their lives to Christ, for God's sake. "When all was sin and shame/A second Adam to the fight and the rescue came."

(2). Secondly, the self offering of Jesus is his perfect submission to the judgment of God upon sin. Unless God is to turn sentimental and to wink at the consequences of sin, there must be a penalty for sin. Christ in his perfect love and bitter suffering bears the brunt of the penalty. He was numbered with the transgressors. He, who knew no sin, became sin for us. Therein lies the majesty and love of the Cross. He paid the penalty of our sins upon the tree.

As the hymn puts it:

> Look, Father, look on his anointed face
>
> And only look on us as found in Him
>
> Look not on our misusings of thy grace
>
> Our prayer so languid and so dim,
>
> For lo between our sins and their reward
>
> We set the Passion of thy Son, our Lord.

By his gracious mercy, he stands in our stead, and by his stripes are we healed. "He loved me and gave himself for me."

(3) The self-offering Jesus is the expression of his perfect penitence for the sins of men.

Some have said: "How can the sinless one offer any penitence for the sins of men?" The truth is that only the sinless Son of God can know the true horror of sin and its shame. For sin blunts the edge of penitence. Only the light can show up the darkness; only Christ, who never fell a prey to sin's entanglements, can ever know its terrible shame. Since we have all felt the attractiveness of sin, we cannot therefore offer a true penitence. But he, who always recognized sin as an insult to God and to man in the image of God, could offer a true penitence on our behalf.

It is the perfect obedience of Christ, the perfect submission to the penalty of sin and the perfect penitence for sin, that form the self-offering of Christ. These things have reconciled us to God the Father. But we have to make them our own. We must come to God uniting our obedience with Christ's; uniting our submission to his judgment with Christ's; uniting our imperfect penitence with Christ's. Then we know that we shall be forgiven by God and restored to fullness of fellowship with him.

The Christian, then, comes to the cross to find out the depth of his tragedy, as sinner who, by his rebellion, crucifies Christ. And there by the perfect self-offering of Christ, he receives the unspeakable joy and gladness of forgiveness. No sacrifice but the sacrifice already made will satisfy God. And the Christian pleads the merits of Christ and is justified by his faith.

And it is this very union of faith in his Savior that enables the Christian to walk in newness of life.

My sermon ends with the story of a great picture. A certain artist who painted pictures for monasteries had for a model a little girl called Pepita. She was a poor, ignorant gypsy child and was curious to know about the paintings in his studio. She stood with her finger in her mouth gazing at a picture of the Crucifixion. "Who is that?" she asked the painter. When he told her about Christ and his sufferings, her little eyes filled with tears. "You must love him very much" she said, "He has done so much for you; what have you done for him?"

The painter was a very religious man and the unconscious rebuke of the gypsy went home. He set himself to paint a great picture of Christ, and he painted it with all his heart. The picture was entitled *Behold the man*. It depicted Christ wearing the crown of thorns, and holding the reed in his right hand. Above it the painter wrote the question of Pepita: "This I have done for thee; what hast thou done for me?"

In time this picture was acquired by the Dusseldorf art gallery. Two hundred years later a Count, Zinzendorf by name, was converted by reading the inscription on the picture. He decided that he could best answer the question by accepting certain Christian refugees from persecution under his wing. He became the patron of the Moravians, who, in turn were to convert John Wesley and set England ablaze with the love of God.

Christ puts that question to you. The answer can only be:

> Love so amazing, so divine
>
> Demands my soul, my life, my all.

THE MEANING OF THE CROSS I

God was in Christ reconciling the world to Himself.
—II Corinthians 5:19

THIS TEXT takes us to the heart of the Christian faith. It reminds us that Christianity is more than a belief in the Fatherhood of God and the brotherhood of man. Its message is more than an assertion that God is the Creator of all things, the origin of all goodness, the power that sustains the universe. Christians believe all these things, of course, but so do Mohammedans and Jews. What makes the Christian faith Christian is the belief that this God has become man; that in the carpenter of Nazareth, the Eternal God has entered this realm of space and time; that as a man he has suffered and died; and that in his suffering and death he has accomplished for us what we could never have done for ourselves. In brief, our Creator is our Redeemer. "God was in Christ reconciling the world unto Himself." At the centre of our holy faith there stands a Cross, the proof of the action of God in time; the pattern of the action of the sons of God.

This text cautions against a common mistake: the misconception that Christ was taking our punishment because God would not forgive us. It is the false idea that Jesus Christ had to persuade reluctance on the part of God to forgive. Dorothy Sayers expresses this mistake in a satirical examination paper she drew up on the Christian faith. It laughs at the common view which misses the meaning of the Cross. The questions and answers are as follows:

> *Question*: What does the Church think of God the Father?
>
> *Answer*: He is omnipotent and holy. He created the world and imposed upon man conditions impossible of fulfillment; He is very angry if these are not carried out He is rather like a dictator, only larger and more arbitrary.
>
> *Question*: What does the Church think of God the Son?

Answer: He is, in some way to be identified with Jesus of Nazareth. It was not His fault that the world was made like this, and, unlike God the Father, He is friendly to man and did his best to reconcile man to God.

Question: What is meant by the Atonement?

Answer: God wanted to damn everybody, but His vindictive sadism was sated by the crucifixion of His own Son, who was quite innocent and therefore a particularly attractive victim.

If this is the common belief about the Cross, is it any wonder that the small boy in the Sunday school should say: "I love Jesus, but I hate God." But what a travesty of the Christian Gospel this is. You will not find on any page of the New Testament a suggestion of any conflict between God and Christ. Didn't Jesus say: "I and the Father are one"? And "Lo, I come to do Thy will." God was in Christ.

The truth is that in Christ God himself was manifest in the flesh. He was a real man like us, but like which of us? He spoke as never man spoke. In his presence men felt the Presence of God, drawing near to them in judgment and mercy, reconciling them unto himself. God was in Christ. That is the centre of the Gospel, which proves the costliness of the love of God. If we would see God's very heart-beats, we shall see them in the Cross.

Have you ever been on a hill-top in a storm? Once I was. The black cumulus clouds were piling up, filling the valley below me with darkness. The landscape soon was blotted out; the sky and land were deep in mourning, and the wind whistled and shrieked like a soul in pain. But suddenly, for an instant, the clouds parted, and a golden arrow of sunlight broke through the dense darkness.

The Cross is like that. At history's darkest point, there breaks forth history's most blinding light. Where sin abounds, grace does much more abound. The occasion of man's blackest crime and deepest degradation, reveals the blazing wonder of God's holy, forgiving, and reconciling love.

I. In the first place the **Cross shows plainly what sin really is**: the attempt to destroy God. It shows evil hurling itself desperately at God's highest revelation of himself. The Christ who proclaimed the spirit of the Lord is upon me, because he has anointed me to preach the Gospel to the poor; he hath sent me to heal the broken-hearted, to preach deliverance to the captives and recovery of sight to the blind, to set at liberty them that are bruised, to preach "the acceptable year of the Lord." He who went about doing good and healing all oppressed by the devil, he who was the very incarnation of the mercy and the love of God, is condemned on a false charge, flogged, tortured, and impaled on a gibbet as a common criminal. See that, and sin is no longer an abstraction, a denial of the law, a mere trespass. It is the tearing of God's body with cruel hands.

A member of an evangelistic campaign invited questions at the close of an open-air meeting. Someone in the audience asked him; "Who crucified Jesus?" Before answering the question, he turned to the crowd and said: "Well who did crucify Jesus?" He got several answers: "The Roman soldiers," "The Jewish mob," "and The priests." These answers we all partly true. But hatred and envy, jealousy and pride, these were the roots of that foul crime, the things that people call little sins: sins of which you and I are guilty almost every day of our lives. It was these, our sins that nailed the Son of God to a Cross.

And that Cross is the mirror in which we must first see ourselves, if we would share the victory and power that it brings. He himself bore our sins in his own body in the tree. We start at the Cross by knowing the desperate evil there is in all of us. There we see sin, in its own dastardly colors, as the diabolical willpower that tries to destroy God.

II. **The Cross reveals** more than the sin of man. We see **God's answer to sin** in a forgiving, suffering love. In the midst of this gross darkness, there shines the glory of God in the face Jesus Christ. The divine love breaks amid the gloom of his persecutors, for he prays: Father, forgive them, for they know not what they do. Calvary tells us that God has taken on his own back the greatest burden of all, the burden of human wrong, and he makes of it the occasion of his forgiving grace. Upon that green hill the cross is brought out of the invisible heart of God into the visible realm of man's sin.

One of the victims of the Armenian atrocities was a girl of about twenty, whose home had been ruthlessly destroyed and her parents shot. Her sisters were spared for the soldiers and the darkish officer kept her for himself. After careful planning she eventually escaped to a British camp, was trained as a nurse, and then sent to a hospital for Turkish prisoners of war. On the night of her arrival as she passed through the officers' ward, the light of her shaded lantern fell on a familiar face, in an instant she saw it all: the homestead in flames, the terror in her mother's eyes . . . And now he was here; he was dangerously ill. A little neglect and he would die, probably in an hour or two. Should she? For a moment she hesitated, and then she dressed his wounds and attended him with the utmost care. Soon the crisis passed and recovery was assured. One day shortly afterwards the hospital doctor brought the nurse to the officer's bedside and said: "But for this girl's devotion you would be dead." "I think we have met before" stammered the man. "Yes," she replied, "We have met before." The doctor had no sooner left the ward than the Turk demanded fiercely: "Why didn't you kill me?" "Because" she replied, "cruelty cannot be righted by cruelty. I am a follower of Him who said, 'love your enemies.' That is my religion."

Bearing sin means that: entering into the fellowship of Christ's sufferings; making evil the occasion of forgiving love. The Cross of Christ gives us a glimpse of God taking upon himself the sin and pain of the world and overcoming evil with good. It is the supreme manifestation of his unchanging, eternal love.

III. Thirdly **the Cross is God's great act of forgiveness**, whereby he reconciles men to himself. The Cross reveals man's sin, God's love; it sets aright a wrong relationship.

For centuries the Jews had looked for a decisive, redemptive act of God. In popular expectation this took the form of political deliverance: they were waiting for the Romans to be driven to the sea. But the prophet Jeremiah, with more penetrating insight, had realized that the human heart, not the arena of nations, was the sphere where God must act. He had foreseen the time when God himself would restore the broken relationship with man:

> Behold the days come, saith the Lord, that I will make a new covenant with the House of Israel, and with the house of Judah ... After those days, saith the Lord, I will put my law in their inward parts, and write it in their hearts; and I will be their God, and they shall be my People ... for I will forgive their iniquity and will remember their sin no more.

Six hundred years were to pass before the meaning of the Prophet's words was realized. Then the Lord Jesus in the night when he was betrayed took the cup, when he had supped, saying, "This cup is the new covenant in my blood." The restoration of this broken relationship, this redeeming Act of God could be revealed only through the death of him who was God manifest in the flesh. "It is necessary" said Jesus, "that the Son of man should suffer many things." Only God himself working through the sufferings and death of Christ could break down the barriers of men's sin and write his law in their hearts.

The Cross confronts us now and commands our allegiance. It calls us to set God at the very center of our life. It calls us to love as Jesus did; to be pierced by sin, to go on loving; to overcome evil with good. It calls us to enter into the fellowship of his sufferings; to offer ourselves a living sacrifice holy, acceptable unto God. Were the whole realm of nature thus redeemed!

THE MEANING OF THE CROSS 2

A Good Friday Sermon, South Africa

God was in Christ reconciling the world unto Himself.
— II Corinthians 5:19

HAVE YOU ever been on a hill-top in a sudden storm? Once I was. The black cumulus clouds were piling up, filling the valley below me with darkness. The entire landscape was soon blotted out; the sky and land seemed to be deep in mourning, and the wind shrieked like a soul in pain. But suddenly, for one unexpected and glorious instant, the clouds parted, and a golden arrow of sunlight broke through the dense darkness. And I was glad.

The hill of Calvary is like that, it is Golgotha—the Hill of skulls—the place of the world's deepest darkness and shame, for this is where men tried to destroy God's Son and our Savior. And yet the disciples of Christ in every age have seen the glory of God in the face of Jesus Christ on his Cross- the Light of the World. The cross which is an instrument of torture and death, and it was a bitterly slow death, is also the sign of our redemption and reconciliation with God. At the darkest point in history, there shines forth the most blinding revelation of God's love in history.

What, then, is the meaning of the Cross?

(1). First, it is a mirror of the dark heart of man. Sin is nothing less than the attempt to destroy the Son of God. The Cross shows us evil hurling itself desperately at God's greatest revelation of himself. Do you recall how our Lord described his own task? "The Spirit of the Lord is upon me, because He hath anointed me to preach the Gospel to the poor; He hath sent me to heal the broken-hearted, to preach deliverance to the captives and recovery of sight to the blind; to set at liberty them that are bruised, to proclaim the acceptable year of the Lord." The beloved healer, teacher and counselor of the people is condemned on a false charge; he is flogged; he is tortured; he is impaled on a gibbet as a common criminal. See that, and you no longer think of sin as chancing your arm, or a white lie, or a trespass. It is the tearing of the Son of God's body with cruel hands. When you realize that, you know that every sin you commit is another nail driven into the holy body of the Son of God, another disappointment to God himself. Face to face with the stark horror of true cross, we can no longer deceive ourselves about the evil that we do. We cannot say: "It doesn't do any one any harm. That is a lie. Our hatreds, our passions, our jealousies, our malice, and our cold superiority, crucify the Son of God anew. The Cross shows us the truth about ourselves—it is cruel that it may be kind. We are all selfish to the core, all in need of a change of heart and spirit.

(2). If we see the sin of man, we can also see here God's answer to sin in a forgiving, suffering, and reconciling love. The Divine love shines through the gloom of the persecutors: "Father, forgive them, for they know not what they do." The Cross tells us that God has taken on his own back, the greatest burden of all, the burden of human wrong. Upon that green hill, the cross is brought out or the heart of God the Father into the visible world of man's sin. The final truth about man is not that he is a crucifier, but he is redeemable. He is an egotist, but he may be a Christian.

It is supremely right that when we think of our Savior on his Cross, the attitude of his scarred hands is an invitation, a welcome. By that he shows that he has linked to himself, by his sacrifice, the soul of everyman, for richer for poorer, in sickness and in health, and death shall never them part. Though we crucify him, he will win us to himself: "I, if I be lifted up, will draw all men to myself." Yes, the Cross is the proof of God's love, signed in the crimson or the blood of Christ.

(3). In the third place the Cross is the pattern of our own Christian life. We cannot escape it. "If any man will come after me, let him take up his Cross and follow me."

We are not here on the surface of the earth to make money, or a name for ourselves; we are here to be conformed to Christ's image, fitted for eternal fellowship with God.

And I take it that this means two things; it means in our daily lives a new understanding of forgiveness, and a new understanding of sacrifice.

Forgiveness. This spirit at its best is illustrated in a story I heard of an Armenian girl of about twenty who was one of the victims of the Armenian atrocities perpetrated by the Turks. Her parents were shot and her home was destroyed. Her sisters were spared for the soldiers and she herself was kept for a Turkish officer. After careful planning, she eventually escaped to a British camp, was trained as a nurse, and eventually sent to a hospital for

The Meaning of the Cross 2

Turkish prisoners of war. On the night of her arrival, she passed through the officers' ward, and the light of her lantern fell on a familiar face. In an instant she saw it all again—the homestead in flames, the terror in her mother's eyes; and afterwards . . . And now he was here; he was ill, dangerously ill. A little neglect and he would die—probably in an hour or two. Should she? For a moment she hesitated. Then she dressed his wounds and attended him with the greatest of care. Soon the crisis was passed and recovery assured. One day shortly afterwards, the hospital doctor brought the nurse to the officer's bedside and said: "But for this girl's devotion, you would be dead." "Y-yes," he stammered, "I-I think we have met before." The doctor had no sooner left the ward, when the Turkish officer enquired: "Why didn't you kill me?" "Because" she replied, "**Cruelty cannot be put right by cruelty.** I am a follower of him who said 'Love your enemies.' That is my religion." How right that she should wear the Red Cross: the emblem of her calling and as the faithful servant of her Savior! That is the kind of forgiveness that we should be showing. . . .

To bear our cross, also means that we **sacrifice** for Christ's sake. Let me give you a profound instance of how one soul responded to the cross. It is told by Sir George Adam Smith, who was the Principal of Aberdeen University, but a very humble Christian also. He was once traveling in a train with a young priest about to sail to West Africa as a missionary. He was going to a land where a white man's life was normally measured not in years but in months. He was on his way to say farewell to his mother for ever on this side of the grave. Adam Smith reasoned with him for some time and agreed that he must give his life whole-heartedly. "But," he added, "Why throw it away? Why not use it for long years in Christ's service? Wouldn't it be better for Christ's sake to think it over again?" Even as the train stopped and the young missionary alighted, Sir George Adam Smith still leaned out of the window and still pleaded with him. The young man simply smiled, then lifted up the Crucifix he wore, looked at it lovingly, and replied: "**He loved me and gave himself for me. And I, can I hold back?**" Tonight, the Risen and Ascended and Glorified Savior with thorn-pricks on his brow, and the spear-prints on his hands and sides, beckons you to follow him in costly care for others, in accepting your share of redemption through facing pain, bereavement, disappointment and loss, in courageous and radiant witness in a time of fear, and you, can you hold back?

If we suffer with him, we shall also reign with him.

THE VERDICT ON THE CROSS

"Gentlemen of the jury" says the Judge, "Bring in your verdict." So says the Greater Judge of all the earth, whose robes are the scarlet of the sunset and the ermine of the clouds. He, the Just Judge to whom we must all give accounts, asks solemnly and presently "What think ye of Christ?" Men and women, weigh your answer carefully, for on your answer depends your soul's safety and peace in this brief life and in the Paradise or Hell beyond it. Weigh this question carefully, for on it depends the future of this nation, of your children and your children's children. Weigh it most carefully, for on it depends the future of Christ's Body, the world-wide church.

What think ye of Christ?

To begin with, stand beside his contemporaries. You will notice that, with the only exception of Caiaphas and the majority of the Sanhedrin whom he had persuaded to kill Jesus, they all bring in a verdict of "Not Guilty." Pilate's better judgment was "I find no fault in Him." Longinus utters the final judgment: "Certainly this was a righteous man."

They declare Jesus innocent, but uselessly. Their true feeling was that in the Cross the powers of evil had claimed their greatest casualty. He was righteous, certainly. He was righteous; but he was crucified. Goodness was murdered on the Cross. The air was thick with the sinister shadows of tragedy. On the road to Emmaus there was no hope, only pathos. "We had hoped that it was He that should redeem Israel." Eternal Love and Eternal Holiness incarnate was mocked, spat upon, reviled, buffeted, pierced, and crucified.

Many men have since taken the same view of the universe, that the fight goes to the strong, that the good man, the sensitive man, the decent man, is trampled underfoot, and Satan stands victor over his corpse, gloating. Thomas Hardy, saddest of all modern writers, shakes his finger in protest at God's treatment of Tess and concludes his diatribe. "The President of the Immortals had ended his sport with Tess." But the disciples had a much deeper anguish and in their agony they could have cried "The President of the Immortals has finished his sport with Christ." They had been mocked, but the most damnable mockery of all was surely the undeserved death of their Lord. Herod's bitter fooling, Pilate's cowardice, Caiaphas's cool hatred, Judas's treachery, were these to have the last word? Were folly, hatred, disloyalty, and treachery the Victors in life's struggle? Was Christ the Victim?

It makes my heart ache to think of the thousands of men and women in this country who come to the first verdict that truth and love and loyalty are casualties in the holy warfare. Pity them, for their lives seem to have been lived uselessly. For them sacrifice is beautiful, but wasted. Their sons and their husbands and their fathers have been taken away from them; they loved them and they lost them. They honor their memories; but a memory does not fill a vacant chair. "If in this life only we have hope in Christ, we are of all men most miserable." There are thousands of people most miserable because their verdict is: innocent, but defeated.

The Cross is a Tragedy and the Crucifixion is for them the supreme example of goodness defeated. The verdict at the cross is in one word "Defeat."

Now turn to the verdict after the Cross, the verdict of the Christian centuries: the pronouncement of the great procession of witnesses. In one word, it is Victory. St. Peter sounds the trumpet first: "Let all the house of Israel therefore know assuredly that God hath made Him Both Lord and Christ, this Jesus whom ye crucified."

St. Paul takes up the strain; "God forbid that I should glory, save in the cross of our Lord Jesus Christ, through whom the world has been crucified unto me, and I unto the world."

St. Bernard sings the same exalting song in his lonely Abbey in Clairvaux. "O Jesus King most wonderful, Thou Conqueror renowned." Eleven centuries later the exultation has not died down.

Charles Wesley repeats the joyous theme. "The name all-victorious of Jesus extol, His kingdom is glorious and rules over all."

John Masefield in his great play *The Trial of Jesus* offers his verdict today. Longinus answers Claudia's question: "Where is He then?" "Let loose in the world, lady, where neither Jew nor Roman can stop his truth."

In the triumphant chorus the church on earth with the church in heaven sings the Hallelujah, the Victory Song: "Salvation to our God which sitteth upon the throne and unto the lamb. Blessing and glory and wisdom and thanksgiving and honor and power and might be unto our God for ever and ever."

Why are they able to speak of the Cross as Victory, of the Victim as the Victor? It is because they are announcing God's verdict. It is because they proclaim the mighty act of God in the Resurrection of Jesus Christ. They have moved from the Evil Friday to Easter Sunday and now they call it Good

The Verdict on the Cross

Friday; the Friday on which our Savior fought the powers of evil and won his victory. They no longer look at a painful crucifix. They see a faithful Christ, faithful beyond death. And they know that death, and sin, and suffering have lost their sting. Death still hurts, sin still damages and destroys, and suffering still racks the frame. But Christ has beaten them and they enter into his victory. They are real crosses, but there are real crowns to follow, "We still have our skirmishes," they say "but he has won the Campaign." It is that knowledge that gives them the morale to go on fighting to the end of their war.

It is not simply the Resurrection that gives them comfort. The Cross itself offers the most tremendous assurances, the assurance of Penitence. There are few of us who are naturally Christian, who have got there from the start. You know only too well, if you look steadily at the Cross, that you are crucifying Christ anew. But he looks at you with the eyes of God. You are poor Peter, loyal one moment and disloyal the next. You are poor Judas—impatient, trying to force the hand of Jesus. You are the frightened disciples sometimes, so afraid of the authorities, barricaded behind the doors of fear. You are poor Mary, seeing the tragedies of life and wondering if it isn't all a waste. You try, you alone know how, you try to live in the serene peaks of faith and loyalty. But, you are often in the darkened valleys of despair.

"Were you there when they crucified my Lord?"

You are there. I am there. And the burden of it might drive us mad, the impossibility of following Christ on every road would be unbearable if we did not know that he understood, that he says even now "Father, forgive them for they know not what they do." There is peace for our nerve-racked souls and calm for our strung-up consciences in that word. "Father, forgive them." We see the exposure of sin there, but we know that he forgives. That is why the Word from the Cross is a gospel and is good news. And the knowledge that he loves and forgives spurs us to greater efforts. If God, through Christ can forgive the Cross, can forgive through the Cross, then, he can forgive, he does forgive you.

Then there is another message of tremendous encouragement. "God so loved the world that he gave his only begotten Son" to share our sufferings and our disappointments. That was love. Nobody who realizes that this was God-in-the-flesh can ever ask again the question. Does God care? The answer is God cares that much. The Cross is the proof. It is a document signed in God's life-blood. Greater love hath no God than this that he lay down his life for his friends. Jesus Christ, God-as-man, did that. It cost him that to redeem us, and it costs him that today. The Cross is a Victory: it is the greatest condemnation of evil the world has ever seen. Innocence, tried and tested, showed up the devilishness of sin. There, villainy is unmasked. The Cross is a Victory: because as we know the love of God and the forgiveness of God, we cross over with Peter and the disciples to Christ's side. Villainy is defeated there. The Cross is a Victory: because God the Father, the Judge of the Universe, wrote unmistakably on Easter Day the words: "This is my beloved Son; this is His Victory." So wrong is righted there.

The Cross is our victory. In this sign, you shall conquer. What think you of Christ? There can only be one answer:

> Blest Savior, we are wholly thine
>
> So freely loved, so dearly bought
>
> Our souls to Thee would we resign.
>
> Love so amazing, so divine,
>
> Demands my soul, my life, my all.

Let us pray: O God, most Holy and yet most forgiving, who doest still suffer in the sins of Thy children, give us penitence for our sins, faith for our trials and eternal life here and hereafter. Amen.

THE MEANING OF THE RESURRECTION TODAY

THIS SERMON is not for everyone. I am speaking directly to two classes of people; the rest of you will be listeners in. I am thinking firstly of the men and women who know the meaning of the word bereavement from personal experience. Those who have seen the firm, cold hand of Death slam the door on the life of a friend or a relation, dearer than life itself . . . I am thinking too of fathers and mothers and wives, whose sons, daughters or spouse are in peril and who sometimes have nightmares when they think of what may happen to them. This sermon is for you.

I am also thinking of another class of people who wish with all their heart that they could believe in eternal life, but find the difficulty too great. And, I add, I honor them for their honesty in admitting the difficulties. I advocate no suicide of the intellect in accepting the Christian faith. This sermon is also for you.

Before the heart can accept any belief and live in it, the mind must grapple with the difficulties. What are the difficulties that stands in the way of a belief in Eternal Life?

1. The first is that many people cannot believe that their lives deserve to survive the grave. They would put it something like this. "I know myself better than any one else does. If I don't think much of it, how can God?" These people think that it would be impertinent to think there was anything immortal in them and even more impertinent to expect God to be interested in preserving them.

What am I to answer? I should say "My friend, I admire your candid humility and modesty. But what you think of yourself is not all-important. Nor is it even important what God thinks of you personally." No man ever won his way into heaven on the strength of his value to God. The passport to heaven bears upon it a cross. God accepts you because of Christ, not because of you. We are justified by faith in Christ, not because of our works. God accepts you for Christ's sake. Faith in Christ is the only requisite. I think you have also forgotten another thing. God is not indifferent to your attempts to obey his will: "God so loved the world that he gave his only begotten Son . . .

that whosoever believes in Him should have eternal life." Eternal life is of God's giving and not of your earning. There was no other good enough to pay the price of Sin.

2. A difficulty that affects other people is this: "People who concentrate on heaven miss the glories of the earth." Heaven seems so to dazzle their vision that they miss the more intimate beauties and wonders of our earthly life.

A friend told Thoreau the naturalist, when he was dying, to turn his thoughts to eternity. Thoreau replied: "One world at a time, brother."

That is the inevitable reply for a lover of nature to make. He refuses to take his mind off the woods, carpeted with the blue and gold of spring's tapestry in the North American woods, to dream of the distant blue of heaven and the remoter gold of the New Jerusalem. He wants to drink to the dregs the wine of this life with its beaded bubbles winking at the brim. This life is all-important to him.

You will never convince the artist or the dramatist or the scientist or the antiquary that their life's work is a mere toy, a mere plaything to while way the golden hours between the darkness of birth and the darkness of death. Raphael will go on painting his glorious scenes in the Chambers of the Vatican, even if you tell him his life is an unreal shadow of eternity. Beethoven will not stop the untiring machinery of his melodic mind, if you bid him remember that only death is real. Shakespeare will go on framing his farewell speech to the theatre in Prospero's adieu, as the curtain goes down on the *The Tempest*, even if you can persuade him he has three more years only to live. The scientists will doggedly persist in his experiments, even though the sands of time are running out. The antiquary delves deeper into the dust of the past, even though the dust of the grave is already settling upon his hoary locks. Why? They all give the same reason: "The work is important and it must go on."

If a realization of their destiny were to hamper their work, I should agree. But the truth is that this world is a moving image of eternity, as Plato described it. The artist, the dramatist, the musician, the scientist, the historian, are all thinking God's thoughts after him. They too now see dimly, but then face to face. Religion need not blind us to earth's values. It should make us more sensitive to them. The religious man is not tone-deaf or color-blind. He should be the most sensitive to the glory of God, seeing that "earth's crammed with heaven and every common bush afire with God."

3. The third difficulty is this. It is claimed that "those whose real hopes are in eternity have been lacking in zeal for progress in time." Those who are

The Meaning of the Resurrection Today

expecting to belong to the New Jerusalem are not anxious to build it upon England's green and pleasant land.

That is what Karl Marx meant when he said: "religion is the opium of the people." Lenin comments on this remark of Marx:

> Religion is one of the forms of spiritual oppression. The helplessness of the exploited classes in their struggle with the exploiters inevitably generates faith in a better life beyond the grave. To him who works and is poor all his religion teaches passivity and patience in earthly life, consoling him with the hope of a heavenly reward. To those who live on the labors of others, religion teaches benevolence in earthly life, offering them a very cheap justification for all their exploiting existence and selling tickets to heavenly happiness at a reduced price.

That was true in Russia, but it is not true in England. The foremost believers in social reform have been Christians: Elizabeth Fry was a Quaker; William Wilberforce was an Anglican as were Charles Kingsley, F. D. Maurice and Charles Gore. Dr. Dale, Dr. Clifford and Dr. Parker were all of them preachers of the social gospel, the authentic voices of the Nonconformist conscience. In this country at least, the church is in the vanguard of social reform.

Now I have tried to deal with the objections to eternal life, let me give you two very short and simple reasons why I believe in eternal life. The first reason is a deduction from human character. The second is a deduction from the character of God.

1. My first reason is the incompleteness of our human life without eternal life. So many of the greatest human lives have been mere torsos—unfinished works of God.

Take Mozart, for instance, who died when he was only thirty-five. Not only was he in the prime of his powers, but he was going to develop them further. I give you the authority of the late Sir Donald Tovey for this. He writes: "in his Requiem, that most pathetic of unfinished moments, Mozart was forming a new style which might have transcended anything we know of him." Take Schubert. He was only 31 when he died. Who can imagine how indescribably lovely the last movement of his *Unfinished Symphony* could have been? Schubert was another unfinished monument of God.

Then there was Keats. He died at the age of 26. What glorious promises he showed. His art might have been a cathedral, but we are left only splendid scaffolding and a rich ruin.

It is not simply the incompleteness of human powers that we experience in this life. We also experience the incompleteness of human love. As an

American minister put it recently: "Love will not believe that Love itself is nothing but ashes and tears."

I refuse to believe that consumption has accounted for John Keats. I refuse to believe that the immortal work of Mozart is finished because he had insufficient nourishment. Mozart's biographer Bacharach tells us: "Music the mainspring of his life, was the last faculty left to him, and still as he lay dying, he continued to puff out his cheeks as sounding the trumpets." I am sure that for him, the trumpets were sounding on the other side.

I am equally sure that the unfulfilled promise of lives given in war will be redeemed and that God will complete his human works of art hereafter.

The very sense of human incompleteness demands eternal life for its fulfillment.

2. My second conviction is that the character of God demands eternal life.

Dr. Carnegie Simpson brushes away all merely theoretical discussion about the future life by saying: "The real question is whether behind all life, not only is there a Cosmic Force which works out impersonal processes of reason, but whether there is one who cares for persons and so cares for them as to care eternally." I am convinced that there is Divine Intelligence behind the Universe, but divine intelligence would have as much interest in my mind as a University professor has in the mind of an idiot. I am equally convinced that behind the universe is a God who cares and who always cares.

That God I know is Jesus Christ. In the outstretched arms on the cross, I see the love that embraces even me and I know that the words "Father forgive them for they know not what they do," are words spoken for me? I know also that the promise "If I live, ye shall live also" is spoken to me, not because of what I have done to deserve it, but simply because he, the Christ, makes it.

It would be blasphemous for me to think of the ruler of the universe as a giant hooper, impersonally conveying the carcasses of humanity to the great refuse-heap of time.

I can only think of God as the beneficent Father who brought Christ again from the dead with the words: "This is my beloved Son," transforming tragedy into triumph.

I am content to believe that he will not cease to care for me as long as there is anything in me that he can care for. My advice to you, in all your anxiety and fear, is to say to the God and Father of our Lord Jesus Christ: "Father, into thy hands I commend my soul and their souls" for time and for eternity.

I will close with this story. A doctor was asked by a dying man, if he had any conviction as to what awaited him in the life beyond? The doctor fumbled for an answer. But before he could reply, there was heard a scratching at the door and the answer was given him. "Do you hear that?" he asked his patient. "That was my dog. I left him downstairs, but he grew impatient and has come up and hears my voice. He has no notion what is on this side of the door, but he knows I am here. Now is it not the same with you? You do not know what lies beyond the door, but you know that your Master is there." For the Christian death is not a cul-de-sac; it is the thoroughfare to the Master, the Open Door. And that softens all blows, and is an anodyne to sorrow.

I BELIEVE IN THE HOLY SPIRIT

THE HOLY SPIRIT

Whitsun Sermon

> *Our Lord: "If you love me, you will keep my commands, and I will ask the Father to give you another Helper to be with you forever, even the spirit of Truth: the world cannot receive him, because it neither sees nor knows him, but you know him, because he remains with you, and will be within you."*
>
> —St. John 14:15–17

AREN'T WE in the situation of the disciples? We believe in God the Father Almighty Maker of Heaven and earth, and in Jesus Christ his only Son our Lord, but do we really believe in the Holy Spirit the giver of life? Is it simply a promise, as it was to the first disciples, or have you really known the fulfillment of the promise in your own Pentecost?

Perhaps you feel like the Japanese convert who was being instructed in the doctrine of the Trinity. Miss Dorothy Sayers tells us that he objected: "Honorable Father, very good, Honorable Son very good, but Honorable Bird, I do not understand at all." He had been misled by the symbol of the Dove, just as other people have been misled by the symbols of the rushing mighty wind, the cloven tongues, and the unfamiliar imagery.

The whole truth is contained in our text: "I will ask the Father to give you another Helper to be with you for ever."

God was invisible, though the creation declared his majesty and power. As the modern telescope reveals his care for the great things, discovering the magnitude of his planning of the stars and planets and microscope shows his infinite care for detail. These are but the outskirts of his ways, the merest hints of his universal design and cosmic planning.

But in Christ Jesus, our Lord, the eternal Son of God, the Word became flesh, and the disciples beheld his glory. That was the world shaking event that happened in Bethlehem, and from which we date our years. The unseen

God became God manifest in the flesh. How slowly did the disciples come to believe this! It was too staggering a fact for them to accept at first. But Peter had glimpsed at the truth in Caesarea Philippi. "Thou art the Christ, the Son of the living God." He said. And Jesus answered. Even Simon had his doubts at the Cross, which only the Resurrection was to quell.

No wonder that when our blessed Lord told his disciples that he was going to leave them, they were mystified. "It is expedient for you that I go away." "I will ask the Father to give you another helper to be with you for ever." This was to be the sense of God within them, the inner monitor and guide.

They were to await his coming. And the promise was fulfilled. They knew themselves to be energized by a power not their own. That is the secret of Pentecost.

God above me—the Creator.

God beside me—the Elder Brother.

God within me—the Holy Spirit.

It was the inward realization of the Spirit of God taking them and using them for the work of our Lord that produced such extraordinary elation and that the men of the world took them to be insane or intoxicated.

I think that many of us are in exactly the situation of the disciples before the cross. We are convinced in an abstract sort of way that God exists—we call him providence or, when we forget, fate or destiny, or when we are highbrow, the Divine Mathematician. He is above, we are here, and we have not made contact.

We are convinced that our Lord was a good man, with magnificent but impracticable ideas. We are dubious about his miracles and we condescend to patronize his teaching because it was really very remarkable that a Galilean apprentice should make such a stir. What is wrong with us? Why this casualness, this vagueness, this reading of every book but the Book of Books? Why this self-consciousness about being a Christian? Why this pride, modern man, why this interminable business with the present world that has choked and suffocated the spirit of God in you?

Why? Why? Because you have not claimed the promise of Christ. Because you have not seen your littleness, your impotence, your brief, busy years against the background of eternity. Because you are of the world, worldly. Because you have closed up the channels of the soul, clogged them with the mud and dung of your possessiveness. Because you have stilted them with doubts.

How can you start? Or, how can you regain the blessedness you knew when first you saw the Lord? On your knees. The life of the Holy Spirit is

The Holy Spirit

a life of prayer. You cannot keep the first fine careless rapture unless you are constantly in touch with God and are acting upon his promptings. That is the experience not only of this poor exponent of God's Word, your minister. It is reassured testimony of the saints from Paul, Perpetua, Martin Luther, and John Wesley to the humblest believers of today. St. Paul declares: "The Spirit itself beareth witness with our spirit that we are the children of God." St Augustine cries "I would not be seeking for Thee, if Thou hadst not already found me." In our time, we need a fresh outpouring of the Holy Spirit, that we may be witnesses to Christ's life.

> And every virtue we possess,
>
> And every victory won
>
> And every thought of holiness
>
> Are His alone.

But the power of the Holy Spirit is not only known to us as individuals. It is not simply by my bedside that I am conscious of his inspiration, clearing away the difficulties, making the impossible possible. The blessed giver of life is known there, but not always, for I am not always receptive to his gracious influence.

It is within the church, in the company of God's chosen people, that he dwells. In the narrative of Pentecost, you notice that they were all together in one place, waiting for his coming.

Let us end on a quote from Professor Victor Murray: "It is noticeable that the disciples, who had lived three years with the historical Jesus and had experienced His love for them, forsook Him and fled, and were capable of the courage of their convictions only when He had gone from them."

THE HARVEST OF THE HOLY SPIRIT

"The harvest of the Spirit is love..."
—Galatians 5:25 (Moffatt)

WHAT IS Christian love? Is it the sense of pity? Let Bismarck answer the question. This man of blood and iron, who spoke of bleeding France white, had a country house with a charming garden. He was so attached to the gardener's kiddies that he played with them and they climbed on to his knees. One of them, a little girl, died. Bismarck went to the gardener's cottage, took the hand of the sorrowing father, and was so touched that he broke into tears. Then he placed a bunch of roses into the hand of the dead child. That was tender, but it was a mere mood, not a habit. It was occasional, not normal. It lacked strength. It was sentiment.

No, Christian love is not mere pity, or else that Iron Chancellor would have been a saint of the modern world. What Shakespeare spoke of love between the sexes, could be applied to Christian love:

> Love is not love
>
> Which alters when it alteration finds,
>
> Or bends with the remover to remove:
>
> O no! It is an ever-fixed mark
>
> That looks on tempests and is never shaken.

It is a constant, sacrificial care.

In this strange language of ours the same word love stands for that selfish-indulgence and that desire to get, which the Greeks called Eros.

If you want to see this Christian and constant love in action in the modern world, read the life of Father Damien, who voluntarily joined a leper-colony as the only way known to him by which to assure the stricken men that he was messenger to them. Or, less spectacularly, think of an Anglican minister who spent Holy Week in the prison cells of Exeter jail, to preach like our blessed Lord himself to the spirits bound in prison.

Or, look into your own experience of Christian men and women, who have borne the most tragic burdens, as the wife continuing to love her husband, when all the neighbors have blackened his name as a scoundrel. She knows it, but her duty to God is to stand by him and how magnificently she does. Parents slaving themselves to the bone to give their children an education such as they never had, receiving only rebelliousness and apathy as a reward, yet continuing to love. That constant, continuous sacrifice is love, real Christian love.

But when St. Paul speaks of love, he means more, much more than this. There were already two words for love in the Greek language. One of them is well-known to you, Eros, because it is the name of the statue in Piccadilly Circus. That Eros was the God of passions; the love that demands. That was not the love St. Paul had known in Christ. There was also another word that stood for natural affection, the relationship of father to son, of mother to daughter, of members within the family for one another, of friends or like-minded folks: Philia. This word would not do to express the extraordinary spiritual love that was the gift of the Holy Spirit and the possession of the new community of Christians. So the Christians coined a new word: Agape.

What was this new love? It was a love such as was exhibited by our Lord, a deep, constant, sacrificial love for the sons and daughters of men, love with the blood-red stamp of cross upon it. That love included Mary Magdalene of the seven devils, and grasped sniveling little Zacchaeus in its embrace. God the son came to earth for that. This was new: identification with men and women as persons, suffering with and for them. This was self-emptying love. The disciples and the apostles knew that God was always like that.

And knowing that God's holy love included the penitent of every race, of every social status, and of both sexes, they were enabled by the Holy Spirit to follow in the footsteps of him who is the Way, the Life and the Truth. And following him, they were able to love the unlovely, to put aside their natural antipathies and animosities; they were able to stamp on the peacock's feathers of pride, even to count like Paul, their own achievements as dung, because Christ had done so much for them.

Time, like a dim haze, softens the rugged features of the landscape, so that even the jagged edges of a rock seen in midsummer seem smoother than they are. We must not let the mists of the centuries blind us to the terrific problems that first Christian community had to face, how jagged were its rocks. Nor must we forget how the Holy Spirit produced terrific fruits of love in them, enabled them, like pioneers, to surmount the jagged precipice to achievement. How the indwelling presence of God welded together into a community men and women who otherwise would have been at one another's throats.

If you want to know how the Holy Spirit of God worked through the Christian community, then see him turn the cesspool of Corinth into a well of water undefiled. A church of God in Corinth! It was like creating a Christian community out of the brothels of Paris! The Holy Spirit did that through Paul and his few assistants.

Canon Cockin enables us to understand this achievement by a useful illustration:

> It is hardly an exaggeration to say that if we were to take religious division as we find it at its sharpest, say between Catholic and Protestant in Northern Ireland, and racial division as we find it at its sharpest, say between Black and Whites in South Africa, and mix them both together, we should get something like the equivalent of the situation which confronted Paul in the eastern half of the Roman Empire . . . The world of the New Testament was "tough" as most situations that our contemporary world could show. And it was out of this world that the Christian Church, the fellowship of The Holy Spirit was created. [Cockin, *The Holy Spirit and the Church*, SCM, 1939, pp. 67–68]

The miracle happened in Corinth. The miracle has happened again and again on the mission-field. The miracle has to happen in the enemy-camp. The miracle has to happen amongst us, in this church. The first and greatest fruit of the Spirit is love, active sympathetic love, not sentimentality or indulgence, but a keen, passionate love for souls.

How can it be done? It can only be done by the aid of the Holy Spirit through us. Of our own strength, even of our own desire we cannot do it. Our prejudices, our snobbery, our condescension, our rootedness in our own private interests are too hardened. If we thought of the rebuffs, the indignities, and the kicks in the face that we should receive, we should not even attempt it.

If our blessed Savior had thought only of the disappointment, the crown of thorns, the cruel nails, the mockery, the spitting in his face, he would not have set his face steadfastly to go to Jerusalem. But he thought of these things as part of the plan of redemption. It was the price he paid for drawing all men unto him.

And we, by the help of God's Holy Spirit, are going to make this church a real community. We are going to look upon men and women as our blessed Lord sees them as souls needing the strength that he imparts, as men and women from whom he died, every bit as much as for ourselves. And that, as far as our church is concerned means the death-knell of pride and snobbery; it means that here under the guidance of the Holy Spirit, we set aside as we enter this house of God, all class distinctions, all differences of dress and we forget any importance we may have in the outside world. We stand on the common ground of disciples of Jesus Christ. All before his holy presence have come short, and all need grace. And together here we pledge ourselves to enlarge our sympathies, as wide as Christ's. The first of the Holy Spirit here shall be love, like the love of God in Jesus Christ that is a self emptying, a suffering love, a sacrificial love, a constant love.

I close by quoting you three lines from a Russian poem. The writer puts these words into the mouth of a highborn lady who followed her husband, a revolutionary, into the Siberian mines. Of him she says "He was more irreproachable than ever / And I loved him as Christ / in his convict garments."

We are called to love all the men and women in our neighborhood as Christs whatever their garments, to weld them into the family of God, the church, by the power of the Holy Spirit.

Let us pray:

Lord God, who hast spoken to us by thy Son himself, who is the brightness of thy glory and the express image of Thy Person, who laid aside his godhead, taking the form of a servant, and being conformed to the fashion of our lowliness, that we might become like him. Enable us by thy Holy Spirit to root out all prejudice and pride that our church may become a true home for souls, a true community of the Spirit, where all worldly distinctions vanish before thee, and we become servants of one another and friends. For the sake of Christ the king of Kings, and yet the Servant and Redeemer of us all. Amen.

I BELIEVE IN THE
HOLY CATHOLIC CHURCH

WHY I BELIEVE IN THE HOLY CATHOLIC CHURCH

You have set me a difficult task in asking me to say why I believe in the Holy Catholic church. It bristles with difficulties. I know that objections to the church are many. But I remember that the founder of the church himself said "The gates of Hell shall not prevail against it." I also recall that the chief critics of the church are not outside but inside, because they have the deepest desire that the church shall be the church without spot or wrinkle or any such thing. But, although I shall defend the ideal of the church, I shall have to admit, as any honest man must, that there have been grievous failures, blots on her pages. In fact, I could almost anticipate all I have to say later by declaring: "I believe in the Holy Catholic church, and I regret it does not exist." But that is only a half-truth. The Holy Catholic church does exist but because it is made up of men and women who are not perfect, it is bound to fall short of the ideal.

Now some of you may not be at all convinced that there is any need of a church. So before I speak or the characteristics of the church of Christ, I must first answer your objections, I think they will be two-fold:

(1) In the first place some of you are saying no doubt that religion is a private affair. It is my concern with God and it is no one else's business. And in saying this you have a great thinker on your side. Professor A. N. Whitehead declared that religion is what a man does with his solitude.

Now that is partly true. You must come to God for yourself; you cannot become Christian by proxy. It is your personal repentance that proves the reality of your religion. We say:

> When I survey the wondrous Cross
>
> On which the prince of glory died
>
> My richest gain I count but loss
>
> And pour contempt on all my pride.

It would be wrong to alter those words to read:

> When we survey the wondrous Cross
>
> Our richest gains we count but loss
>
> And pour contempt on all our pride.

You do not become a Christian until Christ has spoken his condemnation to you in the lonely citadel of your own soul. In that sense, religion is what a man does with his solitude. Or more truly, what God does with a man's solitude.

But do not forget that religion is social and corporate, before it becomes personal. The truth is, as John Calvin put it: "no man can have God as his Father who has not the Church as his mother." Before you became Christian your parents had you baptized, promising that you would be brought up in the fear and admonition of the Lord. You were taught the Christian faith by Sunday-School teachers and if you were lucky, by your parents. And they taught you the Bible, the book which was guarded and translated by the church. If you are a Christian, you are the product of a society. You did not find the Christian faith all by yourself in a corner. You made the response to God yourself; but he was made known to you by the church of Christ.

And religion is social or corporate in another sense. To become a Christian means to belong to a society. You can only continue the work of Jesus Christ in this society. You cannot be a full Christian if you are a freelancer. No more than you could be a star-footballer without a team. God has not willed us to become Christian Robinson Crusoes, living on an uninhabited island surrounded by the engulfing seas of paganism. The Christian life is team-life. It prevents the pride of isolationism and the despair of the individual. It is life in community.

(2). Others of you will paint out to me that the church has failed. You are severely critical perhaps, of the church's attitude towards social questions. You sympathize with the unemployed man at the mission who was listening to a sermon extolling the glories of eternal life. The preacher concluded "and the reward, my friends, will be a golden crown." The unemployed man shouted: "Give us 'alf a crown now."

The church has been too much on the side of the "haves," too unsympathetic towards the "have-nots." I admit it and I am profoundly grateful that the churches are alive to this weakness. But remember also that the slave trade was defeated by a Christian, William Wilberforce, that conditions in prisons were improved by a Christian, Elizabeth Fry; working conditions for small boys were improved by an Anglican vicar, Charles Kingsley. The church

Why I Believe in the Holy Catholic Church

has protested, but it has not protested enough. Do not think her voice has been silent.

Then you may be saying, I can't be attached to any church; I know what scoundrels and hypocrites there are in them! I grant you that there are some; but for God's sake, do not judge the church by its failures. Don't look at Torquemada (the leader of the Inquisition); look at St. Francis. If you want to see the true disciple, look at John, not at Judas. I think we can learn here from the experience of Professor Victor Murray. He says that he was being taken round a famous school by a very grubby little schoolboy (you know the kind: no handkerchief and socks down to the ankles). The schoolboy's heart welled with pride as he said: "We have got six scholarships this year." When asked whether he himself had got one, he replied: "If you want to know what sort of a school this is, for goodness' sake, don't look at me!" In the same way if you want to know what sort of society the church of God is, for goodness sake, don't judge it by the few failures known to you, "If you want to know what the church is, look at St. Paul yesterday and Dr. Albert Schweitzer. If you want to know what it ought to be, look into the face of Christ.

Your argument that the church has failed is only partially true. It has also gloriously succeeded. It is the only organization which in Germany and in Norway stood up to concentration-camps and death. Is that failure? It is the only organization that is breaking the centuries old caste system in India. Can any other organization beat that record?

You still insist that the church has failed. Then what do you propose? To scrap it? But surely that is no solution, that is failure. The solution is to reform it, to let the church be the church, the agency of God. The solution is: come inside, and make it better. Be a creative opposition working from the centre.

I take it that after answering objections, I must now show you what I mean by the words: "I believe in the Holy Catholic church." These words from the Apostles' Creed describe the church, the ideal church, which we all long to see. They show us its distinguishing marks.

(1) The true church first of all is a **divine society**. It is not man-made, it is God-created. It is not an association of like-minded people who say we should like to live this particular kind of religious life and worship in this particular kind of way. History shows us that the church of God was created by God. That is why there must always be a church; that is why "the Gates of Hell shall not prevail against it." It is God's will that it should exist. In fact he created it.

Let me paint two word-pictures for you. Imagine an upper-room in Jerusalem. The door and the windows are barricaded, thin slanting chinks of light reveal a group of men huddled together in terror. Despair and defeat are written constantly across their faces. Their leader has been caught and he is now paying the penalty; he is being slowly crucified on the Hill of Skulls. The game is up; the plans are smashed to smithereens. They are hiding to save their own skins. If the authorities catch them, they will be nailed to a cross.

Now let us consider another picture of the same men: gone are the frowns and fears. They are now standing before the same authorities. When they are told they must be quiet, they cry: "We must obey God and not men," and they carry the message of the Resurrection into the market places and synagogues. They are afraid of nothing and of no-one. What has brought about the change? The Resurrection.

They know that God has proved by this one mighty act that Jesus is the Savior. "Is this wish fulfillment?" did you say. Nonsense! Did the men in the Upper Room in Jerusalem look as if they had the faintest dream or hope of a future for their Leader? But now they know that God has vindicated his beloved Son. The universe is on their side; they are the commanders of a divine invasion. That is the one mighty act: the Resurrection. The other took place when Christ had ascended; it is the sending of the Holy Spirit, the divine spirit who would lead them into truth. These two mighty acts of God formed the Christian church from a defeated remnant of disciples into the spear-head of the church militant. It gave them a divine commission; it put the seal of God upon their fellowship.

That is why I say the church is not the icon of man. It is the product of the mighty acts of God. And its members are those who point, like the Apostles, to the mighty acts of God: in the Incarnation, Atonement, Resurrection, and the Descent of the Holy Spirit. The church was created by God and it consists of those who have been called of God. It is then a divine society. I believe in it because God willed it. I can say that of no other human society. It is unique in being a divine society.

(2) The church is an **undivided society**. That is the second remarkable thing about the church: it is the Catholic or Universal Society, the undivided Society.

Two facts also amaze me about the church. It stretches across space; it stretches across time. Its mighty span reaches across the five continents.

It embraces the pale-faced Eskimo in his igloo and the swarthy African in his kraal. There is in Christ no East or West; no North or South. The divine society knows no geographical or racial boundaries. For Christ has broken down the walls of partition.

But also this great society of the faithful of God stretches over 19 centuries, from the fishermen to the church member who went to her first communion last Sunday. No; it goes back even further, to the beginnings of the race and to the call of Abraham. God had never left himself without witnesses. Can any other society claim such continuity or such range? That, I take it, is part of the meaning of Catholic: ecumenical or world-wide.

But it means more. It means that this divine fellowship is a united fellowship. "United?" you say, scathingly. Well, I can tell you of some of the splits: the Roman Catholics, the Church of England, the Methodists (all three brands of them), the Baptists, the Congregationalists, the Quakers and the Plymouth Brethren. And these are only splits in England. What about all the other countries in the world?

I know about these. And like many another Christian I pray that God will mend and heal our unhappy divisions. But all the same I say that the church of God is united.

The true churches have three essentials in common: a common faith, common sacraments, and a common quality of life. All Christian churches are committed to accepting the Bible as the Word of God and most of them recite the Apostles' Creed, as the summary of their biblical beliefs; they share a common belief. In the second place they observe the Christian sacraments: Baptism and the Lord's Supper. And in the third place, they lead a Christian standard of life.

These are the fundamental signs of unity; many of us long for greater unity of organization that the churches may make combined operations raid on the territory of unbelief. We believe that only thus can our Savior's prayer for his disciples be fulfilled: "I pray . . . that all may be one even as Thou Father art in me and I in Thee, that they also may be in us, that the world may believe that Thou didst send me." That is the goal. But here and now we thank God that we are already united in essentials: the worship through services and sacraments and the same triune God; we believe the same articles of faith; and we aim at the same Christian standards of life. Therefore I say that I believe in the church as a united society. I believe in one Catholic church.

(3) But I have left out one important word: the word **holy**. My third point is that the church is a dedicated society. Or, if you prefer it, a redeemed society.

That is the great necessity for the existence of the church. The convincing proof of its value lies in the daily miracle of conversion. It really does transform beasts and triflers into Christian men; scoffers into saints; Sauls into Pauls. And that inward transformation, I say without any hesitation, is what the world needs today.

Many voices are crying "We need a new plan." Universal education is necessary, but who knows that it will not turn out cleverer devils? A greater equality in income is necessary, but give a poor man a better income and you don't make him into a saint. You may succeed in turning him into a capitalist. Change the system as much as you like, but you will never have a happier world, until you change the man. The selfish brute that unredeemed man is will wreck any system. You must change the wrecker into a reformer if you want the perfect society.

I am reminded of a debate in the University Union in Edinburgh. Speeches were many about the most suitable types of government. It was before the war and young men were tired of democracy. Some wanted Communism, some Fascism, and some Nazism. One student brought the debate to a stirring close with a speech that brought the house down. All he said was "Gentlemen we don't want red shirts or brown shirts or black shirts. I want clean shirts."

As long as the church exists, it will produce the salt of the earth, clean, reliable men with a spotless reputation. If you want clean shirts, you must have a church. Because it is by comparison with Christ that a man is made to feel morally unshaven until he cries like Peter "Depart from me O Lord for I am a sinful man." It is the man who takes that standard that is humble enough to wield power; it is that man who takes as his emblems the towel and the basin—the emblems of service, not of self.

The church I believe in is a holy church of Christ-centered men and women. It is only such that can pull the world into shape again.

Man needs, amidst the conflicting voices of today, divine assurance, a divine society. Man divided into warring camps and warring classes needs a universal, undivided society. Man acquisitive, tyrannical, egocentric by nature, needs to belong to a redeemed and dedicated society. These three fundamental needs are met only by the church which is a divine society, a universal society and a redeemed society. That is why and how I believe in one, Holy Catholic church.

A VICTORIOUS FAITH: CONQUERING RACIAL TENSION

Sermon given at the Congregational Church of Brookfield, Connecticut, July 12th, 1959

> For in Christ Jesus, you are all sons of God through faith. For as many of you as were baptized into Christ have put on Christ. There is neither Jew nor Greek, there is neither slave nor free, there is neither male nor female; for you are all one in Christ Jesus.
>
> —Galatians 3:26–28

THERE SPOKE a man whose fierce pride of ancestry as a Jew had been broken by another Jew, who was also the Eternal Son of God; there spoke a man of towering intelligence, sharpened by the continual cut and thrust of debate who has studied under the greatest religious teacher of the day, Christ excepted; and his cultural and intellectual pride had been humbled so that he counted himself as dung; there spoke a man who had thought slaves inferior and was glad to be the bond slave of Christ because it gave him the greatest freedom; there spoke a man who had regarded women as inferior in all respects to men, and who leant of their amazing devotion to the earthly Christ and saw their continual helpfulness in the Gentile churches. And because his racial, intellectual, class and sexual prejudices had been almost all burnt out of him by his passionate love of Christ for him and all mankind, he gave the church its inter-racial Charter with its two great clauses: 1. You are all God's adopted children because Christ is your elder brother, not of right, not by membership of any race, not because you had a superior education, not because you belong to the weaker or the stronger sex, but simply because he, God, has adopted you.

2. This being the case, we will demonstrate that Christ's new family, the new "Christian race" has overcome racial prejudice, class prejudice, educational prejudice and sexual prejudice.

No wonder the powers of this world cried, as we cry under their influence: "This is revolutionary! Crush it! Away with troublemakers! Crucify them! These are they that have turned the world upside down!" It is still happening... When Michael Scott, an Anglican minister who had worked in the English slums, in the dirt, disease and poverty of India, came into the maelstrom of South Africa, he joined the Indians and the Zulus in a protest march through the seaside city of Durban for fairer laws and treatment; he was taunted by white schoolgirls and their boyfriends: "You dirty white traitor"; he was kicked to the ground and trampled on by the police; he was jailed.

The prejudice of partial Christians still hits nearer home. Three weeks ago, in Columbus, Georgia, the S.W. Presbytery of the Southern Presbyterian Church (a group consisting equally of Presbyterian ministers and Presbyterian laymen) removed Dr. Robert B. McNeill because he preached the Christian Gospel according to St. Paul. The Christian Century of this week (July 8th 1959) reports that he has had a serious heart attack. Because he fought the good fight of faith for you and me. And, thank God, the Moderator of the Presbyterian Church of the South and many, many of its ministers are humbled.

Of course, we say, "That was down South. They were Presbyterians. They're not Northerners as most of us are. They're not Congregationalists, as most of us are." Listen, before you comfort yourselves with such illusory veils that only show your pride more markedly. Only a few months ago, the Revd. Mr. Fred B. Manthey, pastor of the Congregational Church of Levittown, Pennsylvania, was kicked out of his charge because he advocated integration in the church, and wanted it to be a demonstration of Christ's community-creating.

When my brother for whom Jesus Christ died, suffers insults, and the Jews and the Negroes and Africans are the races that Christians (so-called) have insulted most in the modern world, when my white brethren who are suffering for Christian color-blindness are jailed or have heart-attacks or are kicked out of the ministry, I am insulted; but more, this nation is insulted and supremely God is insulted. We are spitting in the face of the Son of God, mocking his Gospel of confidence and trust, crucifying him anew.

What is wrong with us? 1. First it is a failure of imagination. Take anti-Semitism: we lump the Jews together as a race. With courtesy we call them "Hebrews" with naked crudity we say with curled lips 'Yids'. Next time, recall Jesus was a Jew, Paul was a Jew, Peter was a Jew, Einstein was a Jew, Ann Frank was a Jew, and Arthur Miller is a Jew. JESUS was a Jew.

A Victorious Faith: Conquering Racial Tension

2. Let a great dramatist help you feel what it is like to be a Jew, in this case from *The Merchant of Venice*. The man had gained financial security, but was a widower and had lost the love of his daughter to a young nominal Christian:

> I am a Jew! Hath not a Jew eyes? Hath not a Jew hands, organs, dimensions, senses, affections, passion? Fed with the same food, hurt with the same weapons, subject to the same diseases, healed by the same means, warmed and cooled by the same winter and summer as a Christian is? If you prick us, do we not bleed? If you tickle us, do we not laugh? If you poison us, do we not die? And if you wrong us, shall we not revenge? If you are like us in the rest, we will resemble you in that. –If a Jew wrongs a Christian, what is his humility? Revenge. If a Christian wrong a Jew, what should his sufferance be by Christian example? Why, revenge. The villainy you teach me I will execute.

Another writer, in our own day has enabled us to look behind the mask of the Negro we normally see, and find there a man like ourselves, overcoming the confused bitterness of his heart. Though a minister, his son is to die for complicity in a murder, the murder of a white social welfare expert who had given his working days for the betterment of the Africans. It is of course Alan Paton's *Cry, the Beloved Country* I refer to, which made a fine film and a superb musical, *Lost in the Stars*. Here is the complete material for tragedy, for the white father whose son was killed, and for the African minister whose son is to die. If ever two men had reason to hate one another in the land where racial prejudice and fear clutch like a fog at the throats of men, it was these two. True, they were both Christians the African pastor was a real man of faith, but this event shook his faith. The white South African farmer was a good member of the white church, decent to the Africans who worked on his lands—paying them never a penny less than the usual pittance, and seeing that if they were sick, they got the medicine to make them fit to work for him. To Kumalo, Jarvis senior is a superman made of iron; to Jarvis senior, Kumalo is a nice ignorant little minister. When the tragedy strikes, each becomes bitterly suspicious and hostile. Kumalo thinks, "You cannot trust these white men. They, with the gold they dug out of Johannesburg and the better pay they give the miners, lured my soul away from home, made my sister a prostitute." Jarvis senior must have thought: "Give these niggers an inch and they take a yard; my boy thought they could be reformed through his social work. What did he get for it? An early death."

Yes there is desolation in the novel. No wonder Paton cries and cries out upon his beloved country! But its sub-title is *Comfort in Desolation*. After the deaths of their sons, the basic truth is that they are both fathers without sons, both bereaved fathers. And the comfort comes from realizing in their agony that hate is destructive and love is creative, because it is forgiving and that God also lost his Son, crucified by prejudice. Yes there was the comfort of the Gospel of the Cross and the promise of life everlasting in this novel. But there was also a deep warning.

A very wise African minister (who is a member of the Community of the Resurrection to which Father Trevor Huddleston belonged who wrote *Naught for your Comfort*) asks the white men and women: "What if they should have turned to loving, when we have turned to hating?"

The great Greek tragedian Aeschylus said: "It is by suffering we learn" (*pathei mathos*). A remarkable contemporary theologian, Dr. Reinhold Neibuhr, has said "On earth, love will always be suffering love." But a greater than Aeschylus or Niebuhr declared: "Blessed are ye when men curse you and revile you and persecute you, for great will be your reward in heaven."

It is clear that we have a failure of imagination and also a failure in discipleship.

But there are churches, in many parts of the world, where classes and races have been overcome and men, women of white, black, brown and yellow races are one in Christ Jesus.

Brookfield, Connecticut, 1959

WANTED: OUR OWN PENTECOST AS A COMPANY OF THE CHURCH OF CHRIST

Ye shall receive power when the Holy Ghost is come upon you.
—Acts 1:8

WHAT WE want is power...

There is nothing more disappointing than a great structure which needs power. I saw such in Clydebank, Scotland in the great shipbuilding yards of John Browns in the year 1934, I believe it was. Towering over the houses of the unemployed was this symbol of their despair—the gigantic 534, in which the skill of naval architects and engineers, the brain and brawn of the foundries, the sweat of the colliers deep under the earth, and the precision of the riveters and the interest of their wives and children, seemed to have been wasted. This great hulk of a ship lay for years dominating the skyline of their lives. Some years later, I saw it being launched on halide. And four years ago, I sailed back from New York to Southampton on the 534, as thousands of men did during the war years. But then, it was known as the Queen Mary. In the meantime, the depression had lifted and the ship had been launched by the grace of God and the cooperation of men, and her great turbines pulsate with power.

The church is a great structure that has weathered many storms under her great Commodore, Our Lord Jesus Christ, and her captains have often been saints, and her company saints. But Judas and Demas have been of the company too. I believe that the great ship of the church—or if you like to think of it as a flotilla of ships, each denomination a ship, and each eight hour watch, a different congregation or company of Christ's people—I believe that the church of Christ and the churches are ready to make a new voyage. There are signs of this all over the world—in Russia e.g. among the Baptists, in England, among all the companies of Christ almost, there is new hope rising. And if it is, not to be a false hope. We must have **power**.

What are the conditions for receiving power? Remember that it is God's power—the inner power of the Holy Spirit that we each need, and our churches all need, that the turbines that were still may start moving again.

First and foremost, there is **prayer.** The disciples were promised that they should receive this power from the ascended Christ, just before he left their visible presence, and they should then be his witnesses in the place of their failure—Jerusalem, and from there go outwards to Judea—the whole of Palestine, then to the North, and from there to the ends of the earth. And this happened, as the book Acts of the Apostles shows: some stayed where they were to witness; some like St. Paul, went through the Mediterranean area; and their successors took the Christian Gospel and the Christian community, the church, to the end of the earth. But they had to wait and they had to pray. Acts 1:14 speaks to men and women: "These all with one accord continued steadfastly in prayer." Christ is the proof of God's love and prayer is one of the proofs of our love for him.

Secondly they went through the **election** of a new deacon. They picked another deacon to take the place of the traitor, a very undramatic thing to do. But it was important enough, for he was a minister and an apostle, one who served the community of Christians with his gifts and a witness to Christ. Pentecost is a call to the officers to remember their calling.

II. The Results of the Coming of the Holy Spirit on the Waiting Community of Christians

Firstly, they had **courage** in the place of their defeat. Peter stands boldly; the Coward proves his commissioning to be from Christ. They had courage to face the sneers of men, who had a nice smart worldly reason for explaining all the enthusiasm. "They are just tight," was the wisecrack. They are "round the bend" is what some think of Christians who take their calling seriously today. But Peter lifted up his voice and preached to the people that the crucified Christ was the risen Lord. Israel's Messiah and the world's, now at God's right hand, has received the Father's promise and poured forth the power that your are witnessing. Courage to witness openly, and to win men through the Holy Spirit's power for Christ.

Secondly they created a genuine Community, united by the Holy Spirit, whether in the Temple or at home in these ways:

Wanted: Our Own Pentecost as a Company of the Church of Christ

a. a real sharing of their goods and gifts, parting with what they had, as men had need of them (Acts 2:44–45).
b. the instruction of the apostles in teaching.
c. the breaking of bread in communion.
d. prayers in worship.

Lord, revive thy church by and with me.

WANTED: A PERPETUAL PENTECOST

The fellowship of the Holy Spirit be with you all.
—II Corinthians 13:14

St. Paul is sending birthday greetings to the church at Corinth, to every church, reminding them that the church is a fellowship of the Holy Spirit, in origin and in continuance. Later, I shall speak of one side of the church's essence: that it is a fellowship of Christians united by the presence of the Holy Spirit in its midst. Now, I want to speak of the other side of its life. It is a fellowship of separate souls with God! There can be no such thing as a fellowship of believers, unless there has first been a fellowship of individual souls with God.

Do we need this reminder? Of course, we do. Without the presence of the Spirit of God, in the souls of members, the church becomes a human museum, a collection of stuffed-human beings, dead. It was the spirit of God breathed into the body of Adam that made him a soul; it is the continual in-breathing of the Spirit of God that keeps our souls alive. Without the Spirit, we have the form of men and women, the shape of human beings, but we are only highly complicated animals. God is as necessary to our spirit, as air is for our lungs, or food is for our bodies. Yet, who would dare to say that the majority of Christians today are indwelt by the Holy Spirit?

Compare us with the disciples at Pentecost and we are only shadows of it those God-inspired men. We are not spiritually alive. That is why on Whitsunday, the Christian churches in all their branches, look back to the rock whence they were hewn, wistfully trying to recapture the lost glory of the infant church.

Some weeks ago we went for a walk to the Old Church, as it is affectionately called, in Shanklin. We reached it by walking past a group of old-world thatched cottages, leaving behind the solid grey-stone Victorian boardinghouses. In the church-yard, the sun picked out the inscriptions on old tombs and tomb-stones. The interior of the church was cool and dark and empty but for us. On a side-table was the customary book for visitors, who scrawled their signatures rapidly, glanced at the architecture, and rushed back into the sunlight. It was beautiful as a monument to a vanished past, but it was the reposeful beauty of death! It was an empty church, a church in a graveyard, a church which modernity had left in a backwash of history, building its town in a new quarter, a church of inner darkness, a church of spectators. It was, alas, a typical church, a church from which the Lord, the Giver of Life, had departed: a museum-piece.

As I looked at the fading, moldering notices in the porch, I wanted to put up a large notice for all to read. And this is what it would say: **Wanted: a new Pentecost! Wanted: the Holy Spirit in the hearts of the believers!**

And the same needs to be written over every church in England, for there is only a faithful remnant in each that is God-empowered, driven by the dynamo of the Holy Spirit. I see everywhere lives that should be Christ surrendered, souls that should be blossoming for God, and bringing forth the fruits of the spirit. What are they? They are pressed petals in a botanist book, preserved-fruits bottled in a dark larder! The communion of the Holy Ghost be with you all! That is it! The life-giving energy of Holy Spirit be in every slumbering soul, stabbing it awake, keeping it loyal, and making it a daring and confident witness for God! Like Ezekiel, we cry: "How can these dry bones live?" And the answer is: "I will put my spirit in you and ye shall live." This is the promise that shall renew us and the life of our dying churches in the world.

But how? But how? God will perform it, but we must be prepared. We must be ready as the men at Pentecost were. And I want you to notice two simple things about them, simple but decisive. First, they were men of great expectation and eagerness. Pentecost did not happen in a vacuum. It took place in an atmosphere where faith and eagerness had led the way. This revolutionizing spiritual experience happened to men who were listening for God. And without that there will not be a Pentecost either for the individual soul or the church.

So it has always been: God cannot breathe this Spirit into our souls, unless they are eagerly waiting for it. The news of the coming of the Messiah came to Simeon and the little praying group in the Temple. The news of a Reformation of a corrupt and dying church came to Martin Luther, as he waited for the Scriptures to speak their message to his soul. The news of the missionary reawakening in the 18th century came to William Carey whose motto was: "Expect great things from God." It cannot come to men and women who are bored, apathetic, and listless and without hope. I believe that there is a great spiritual experience awaiting every man or woman who will rise up and receive it. I do not see how we can believe in the Christ of the New Testament without believing in that. But it is we who baulk God by our indifferent or cold or cynical attitudes. Let me put it this way: if I offer up my prayers by rote, as a kind of duty that had better be got through, a custom, I am taking the channel between God and myself that Jesus Christ has dug with his own hands, and blocking it. But if I offer to God a prayer electrically charged with faith in the hushed shrine of my secret soul, then I am expecting God to speak and listening for it, and God will speak. I know it because he has done it. And you know it, because he's done it for you. The Holy Spirit comes to the expectant heart that has faith in him.

Then will you notice a second thing about these men who had the great experience. They were Christ surrendered men. Every one of them had given up himself to Christ up to the hilt, was ready to go anywhere, attempt anything at Christ's command.

Is it there that our difficulty lies? Let me be quite blunt and honest here. Not one of us has a right to complain that God gave these men spiritual experiences he has never given to us, if we have never gone the lengths with Christ that they did. We have no right to that experience unless as we have taken the circle of our life and lifted it bodily off the center called self, and set it down on the center called Jesus. Pentecost is God's answer to a soul who has surrendered to Jesus; it comes after the surrender, not before.

Now, that is our trouble. We want God's Spirit without God's conditions. Isn't that true of our day-to-day life? How often we are faced with moral decisions and how often we go on arguing about it? What we don't do is to say: "God has given his orders: there is an end to it. There is no need for argument." It is so much easier to spend half a dozen hours discussing religion, than half an hour obeying God.

Make no mistake. We have those marching orders in the Ten Commandments and in the example and teaching of Jesus Christ. But we will not study them daily. Discuss them we may, but obey them, we will not.

Isn't that the root and reason for our failure? Dr. J. S. Whale puts this vividly and with practical truth when he writes:

> instead of putting off our shoes from our feet, because the place whereon we stand is holy ground, we are taking nice photographs of the Burning Bush from suitable angles; we are chatting about theories of the Atonement with our feet on the mantle-piece, instead of kneeling down before the wounds of Christ.

Our Lord said to his disciples "Follow me," not discuss me, think about me, debate me, but "Follow me." And this is the test of whether we really love Christ, the test of obedience. "If you love me, obey my commandments." "Love and obey, for there's no other way," as the fine old hymn puts the command of Christ. The human agents of Christ's church were obedient, tarrying in Jerusalem until the power came from on high. They acted just as they had earlier, when they had left their nets or their place at the receipt of custom to follow Christ.

We cannot have the gift of the Holy Spirit until we are Christ-surrendered. As Dr. James Stewart expounds it:

> Christ does not court any man. Christ commands him. And Christianity does not consist in complimenting Christ as genius or artist or poet or teacher or social reformer or anything else. It means bowing to Christ as commander. It is being ready to make His will our law, His commands our joy, and its hardest marching orders the music of our life.

I have been reading a moving tribute to his son "Geoffrey" paid by his father in the memorial to this young commando. The book entitled *Geoffrey* contains a number of letters that the boy sent home, during his year of active service. One of them tells how he felt when he volunteered for a Commando Post. He wrote:

> It's the grandest job in the army that one could possibly get, and is a job, if properly carried out, that can be of enormous value. Just think of operating under direct orders from the C-in-C. No red tabs, no paper work, none of all the things that are so cramping and infuriating. Just pure operations.

I want to apply those words to the young people who are today being received at Christ's table as associate members of the church. You are entering into the grandest job in the Christian army, volunteering for service with the King of kings. You are operating under direct orders from the Commander-in-chief, Christ. Your task is as pure operations.

Obedience in Bible-reading, worship and private prayer to the marching orders of Christ will make you Christian commandos, directed by the guidance of the Holy Spirit in your hearts.

I want to end on a personal note addressed to all of you. If I could count the greatest success of my ministry under God, it would be that I had persuaded my people to read a chapter a day of the Scriptures, with a word of prayer at the end of it, as a promise of obedience to God's marching orders. If I could only do that, I should not be afraid of them slipping away when a change of the ministry came. I should not fear for their soul if they moved away from the neighborhood. For I should know then that the church was alive, hearing and obeying the Holy Spirit and I should know that Pentecost has come with great power to this church.

CHRISTIANITY AS THE SERVANT CHURCH

Changes in Religion in the 20th Century

THERE HAVE been kaleidoscopic changes in religion and art in the twentieth century, so that it is difficult to try to obtain perspective in either section of our interests. Consider, for example, the successive fashions in theology in the 20th Century:

1) The Social Gospel in the USA and the New Theology in Britain (Rauschenbusch and Campbell).

2) Uniting constructions, stressing the closeness of one denomination to another with the increasing impact of the Ecumenical Movement in the Faith and Order and Life and Work commissions from Edinburgh (1910) onwards. For instance Catholics and Lutherans agree on all but the role of the papacy.

3) The rediscovery of mysticism and Religious Phenomenology with, for example Dean Inge, Evelyn Underhill, Baron von Hügel, Rudolf Otto and Van der Leeuw.

4) Incarnationalist Theology: Gore and Temple

5) Dialectical theology or the Theology of the Word of God in Karl Barth and Emil Brunner, as the forerunners of so-called Neo-Orthodoxy, and also with Kraemer. This led to the facetious "Thou shalt love the Lord thy Dodd with thy Barth and thy Neiebuhr as thyself.

6) Demythologizing Theology (Bultmann).

7) Philosophical Theology as Correlation (Tillich).

8) Radical secular-oriented Theology (as in Bishop John A. T. Robinson's Honest to God) and revolutionary theology of the 'God is dead' group with Altizer, Van Büren, Gabriel Vahanian and William Hamilton, beginning with Bonhoeffer and going on to Harvey Cox's Secular City.

9) Three current varieties are (a). Liberation (b). Hope and (c). Play.

Artistic Techniques in the 20th Century

The successive techniques of artists in the 20th century have been equally bewildering, as successively we consider: 1) post-impressionism, 2) symbolism, 3) vorticism, 4) cubism, 5) surrealism, 6) functionalism 7) abstractionism, 8) "Pop," 9) "Op" art.

Corrolation of Religion and Art in the 20th Century

To attempt a correlation of nine types of theology through nine pairs of artistic spectacles would lead to eighty-one possible solutions and that would be the work of a computer not a theologian or an art critic. To deal more generally with religion, rather than the various alternative theologies, it is appropriate to ask: What have been the major movements in western religion in the 20th century and how far are these reflected in its art and architecture? These 5 movements are ultimately indiscociable but they must be considered separately and successively.

Ecumenical. I shall mention first the Ecumenical Movement, because it has been the impetus to many of the other movements and it is a remarkable fact that if nineteenth century Christianity was competitive Christianity, twentieth century Christianity is cooperative and uniting, i.e. ecumenical Christianity with the creation of the World Council of Churches in which Protestant churches and the Eastern Orthodox churches were united in Amsterdam in 1948, and there have been Roman Catholic observers. Then the Second Vatican Council has had Protestant and Orthodox observers and only in December 1965 was the five hundred year old schism between Catholicism and Orthodoxy healed. The implications of ecumenism for art are very great, because divided churches will no longer be suspicious of one another's traditions in religious architecture and art and will borrow freely, just as already the Episcopal and Lutheran churches have acted as cultural bridge churches between Catholicism and left-wing Protestantism, as seen in the departure from iconoclastic Puritanism in Congregational and Presbyterian churches. The ecumenism and eclecticism of the future are likely to be far greater. The Christians have a greater concern for Jews and for Buddhists in studying techniques of contemplation.

Liturgical. Since 1840, there has been an important Liturgical movement, which is stressing the corporate adoration of the church as the clue to renewal and reformation of the church. The emphasis here is on intelligibility and understanding in worship, a Basilican posture, the vernacular tongue; the community offertory, and a comprehensive interpretation of the Eucharist as eucharist, communion, sacrifice, eschatological banquet and commemoration. As worship is rethought, so is the architecture and symbolism of the church: is its chief purpose functional or symbolical; horizontal or vertical; monumentality or service?

Biblical. Worship is the context in which the Bible becomes contemporary witness. In the Ecumenical movement it is increasingly felt that traditions divide and it is in a common approach to our primary document, the Bible, that we shall attain unity. So the new biblical movement, with a historical and theological approach, is felt to be important. This time it is the open Bible for Catholic and Protestant alike.

Social. The Social Reform Movement is a great and growing concern within the contemporary church, though it has been with us since the "Social Gospel" was proclaimed at the beginning of the present century. In America today, it takes the form of Civil Rights protests and a concern for greater social and economic justice. There is a deep criticism of any privilege for the church and a demand that it justify itself as the servant church. The ethical justification for Christianity becomes as strong as the theological justification weakens. And I believe that what is happening at present is very well represented in Bishop Robinson's *The New Reformation* in which the Christ Community is pictured as needing to live as the servant or slave of Christ who is now interpreted in terms of "The Man for Others." Bonhoeffer wrote:

> The Church is her true self only when she exists for humanity. As a fresh start she should give away all her endowments to the poor and needy. The clergy should live solely on the free-will offerings of their congregations, or possibly engage in some secular calling. She must take part in the social life of the world, not lording over men, but helping and serving them. She must tell men whatever their calling, what it means to live in Christ, to exist for others. [*Letters and Prayers from Prison*, London, 1955, p. 124, cited by JAT Robinson. *The New Reformation*. p. 27]

In the past the church has been an institution alongside, not the leaven within, the world it meant to change. The real difference between the old Reformation and the New Reformation is the different basic questions they are asking. "How can I find a gracious God?" This question drove men to search desperately for an answer. A different question haunts us also. It agitates entire nations. It makes us in turn victims of anxiety and despair. "How can I find a gracious neighbor? How can we somehow live at peace with one another?" (*Ibid.* Robinson, 32).

Christ as the man for others. The new emphasis must be on the humanity of God. The start must be from John 14:9: "He who has seen me has seen the Father." And the Father is seen in the Incognito of the Son in the parable of the sheep and the goats, i.e. in term of the gracious neighbor. He is not the pre-existent Christ but the pro-existent Christ—the one who exists for others.

The Christ as the accepting and servant community. In the days of the Reformation and Counter-Reformation, the church was defined as a closed circle, gathered from the world, a fortress, or lighthouse above the storms instead of in them. Now the church has to be redefined as the people of God in the structures of the world, manifesting Christ in serving the world. It is to be a holy secularity, not set apart, but sent serving into secularity. Gibson Winter sees the church neither as the cultic organism of the Middle Ages nor as the confessional fortress of the Reformation and Counter-Reformation period but as a prophetic fellowship being the only relevant form of "the servant church in a secularized world." Christ is the Man for others; the church is men and women for others. This is the suggestion of the central Christian affirmation of the Incarnation where we see the "Supreme as Servant" (W. Temple), God for man (K. Barth).

Charismatic. The charismatic movement runs through all denominations of Christians, including the Roman Catholics. It is a strong protest against the impersonality of vast churches and against middle-class respectability, racial prejudice and compromise on the part of many Christians.

It emphasizes supernatural phenomena such as speaking in tongues (glossoramenia) but more importantly "sharing" religious virtues in small affectionate groups gathered together for Bible study, prayer and mutual support as in the early church days.

I BELIEVE IN THE
COMMUNION OF SAINTS

ALL SAINTS' DAY

Beloved of God, called to be saints.
—Romans 1:7

CALLED TO be saints? Not me, says Tommy Atkins. "No fear." We have Kipling's word for it:

> Oh it's Tommy this and Tommy that; an' Tommy go away;
> But it's "Thank you Mr. Atkins" when the band begins to play;
> It's Tommy this an' Tommy that and Chuck him out, the brute
> But it's the Savior of 'is country when the guns begin to shoot;
> Then it's this and Tommy that and Tommy ow's your soul;
> But it's thin red line of 'eroes when the drums begin to roll;
> We aren't no thin red 'eroes, nor we aren't no blackguards too;
> But single men in barricks, most remarkable like you;
> An' if sometimes our conduct isn't all your fancy paints
> Why single men in barricks don't grow into plaster saints.

They don't grow into plaster saints and what's more, they don't want to. What are they afraid of? It's the hall and the pedestal. Modern man doesn't mind being good; but he positively loathes the idea of being pious. Saints without hales; saints without pedestals. That's more in his line.

If the stained-glass saint is at a discount, we need not worry if fashions in sainthood have changed. St. Simeon Stylites is not popular today. If the medieval mind was stupefied with admiration at this holy man who sat for years unmoved upon a stone pillar so long that the vermin fell off his skin; modern minds say "What an egotist and cheap exhibitionist!"

Many of the stories of the saints make pleasant and edifying reading, but we would no more think of imitating them today than of throwing paraffin on an incendiary bomb that had lodged in our attic. The only one of the medieval saints that attracts us now is St. Francis. And that is because he is so modern. He stepped off the pedestal and came to life. He quitted the cloister for the company of men. He left the monastery for the mob. Ask a man of today for his collection of saints and he will roll off the names of Albert Schweitzer, Sir Ronald Ross and Grenfell of Labrador. These are the saints without haloes; this is religion and life, not religion running away from it.

It is the custom, in communions which keep All Saints' Day, to remember with reverence the names of distinguished saints; might it not be more fruitful for us to remember the unremembered and undistinguished saints?

I sometimes think that the perfect place to celebrate All Saints' Day is Mansfield College Chapel which was described by Dr. Heiler as "The most Catholic place in Oxford." Lift your eyes above the gothic pillars and around you are the most varied collection of saints. There is your favorite, St. Francis; there also is St. Monica, the mother of St. Augustine; these are familiar figures. But as your eye travels towards the Western door of the Chapel, there appear unexpected figures: there is John Bunyan, David Livingstone, William Penn and John Wesley: sainthood up to date.

But what I like most of all are two figures in a little window to the left of the choir stalls. In it are just a Victorian woman and her husband. She is wearing the grave, long dress of her period; he has the frock-coat and the inevitable side-boards of the era? Who are they? I haven't the least idea. I should call them Mr. and Mrs. Anonymous Christians. They are the unpedestalled saints that St. Paul had in mind when he wrote to the church folk at Rome, telling them they were the beloved of the Lord, called to be saints. He had in mind Mr. and Mrs. Anonymous Christian. I suppose he would have laughed rather sadly if he had entered one of our churches and seen his battered body, his unattractive face beatified into an athletic figure, radiating piety. This was a man who had no pretensions to extraordinary saintliness. He hadn't reached the stained-glass window stage. "I press on," he still had a long way to go.

It looks as if what St. Paul meant by sainthood and what the medieval church meant by it, were very different ideas. Sainthood for St. Paul meant two things: 1. the recognition of the call from God; 2. the proof of the call witnesses by a sanctified life.

We may say that the two chief virtues of the saint are humility and holy service: self-denying service.

I. Humility, I am certain, is the truest test of a real Christian. Not the mock humility of a groveling Uriah Heap, a smarmy humility or a faked humility, but a genuine reliance upon God. That is the hard lesson to learn.

All Saints' Day

Dr. A.D. Lindsay in his book: *The two moralities*, writes: "There is a sense in which no man is a Christian, the paradoxical sense that a man is a Christian only when he acknowledges that he is not completely one." It is only when pride comes before a fall, when I am tripped up by my conceit and sufficiency, that I put my hand into the hand of God.

I am reminded of the Sunday School Teacher in New York who gave a long and interesting talk on the Pharisee and Publican and ended by saying: "And now children, let us thank God we are not like this Pharisee." This attitude is flat denial of our faith. No saint ever gatecrashed into the kingdom; he found his way there by climbing up its spiral stairway on hands and knees. And he muttered, as he reached the top: "I who am the least of saints."

That is the first hall-mark of sainthood: a dependence upon God, not a frightening self-sufficiency. The doctor cannot help the patient who harangues him and who tells him how to cure himself; in the same way, God cannot make a saint of a man who has a private formula for his own perfection. Only those who are sick need a physician, says our Savior. Humility is dependence upon God is the first mark. St. Paul reminds us that we are called to be saints. His grace meets our need; his hand lifts us out of the ditch. We cannot but he is able.

II. The second mark of sainthood is self-denying service. I do not care to imitate the man who was so concerned to be right with God himself that he could ignore the world. No St. Simeon Stylites for me; give me St. Francis as my model.

Ever eloquent Milton speaks to my need: "I cannot praise a fugitive and cloistered virtue, unexercised and untreated, that never sallies out and seeks adversity, but slinks out of the race, where that immortal garland is to be run for, not without dust and heat."

I want to proclaim Christ not in a cloister, but in a crowd; not in the clean, cold, remote part of a monastic cell, but in the dust and heat of everyday life. And how I envy some of you your opportunities of proclaiming an unprofessional Christianity!

We have desperate need today not for the Christian publicity expert, but for the anonymous Christian. My heart warms as I think of the unsung heroes of our faith; the unspectacular saints. I recall with pride the tinkers, tailors, farmers and housewives who made up the unpretentious majority of our first puritan congregations in this country. Who knows their names?

The names of most of them are forgotten. Their names have been obliterated from the slate of time and the passage of the years, the fate of all self-denying saints. Who knows the names of the saints, the beloved in the Lord, who were in Nero's household in Rome? Who knows the names of the first missionaries to this country—the earliest Celtic Missionaries? Who can tell you the craftsmen who in their guilds built our storied cathedrals? I see no trade-marks on the windows; no initials on the fan-traceries; no monograms on the richly carved woodwork. Who can tell me the author of that lovely carol: "God rest you merry gentlemen?" Who wrote "The first Noell the angels did say?" The answer in every case is: Mr. or Mrs. Anonymous Christian.

And on this I praise God for those unknown saints who by faithful anonymous service, fought the good fight in the ranks; subscribed to the church of God without letting their right hands know what their left hand was doing; painted, wrote, composed, lived, helped, giving glory to God. I thank God for the famous saints; for the extraordinary splendor of their lives; but I remember the unknown warriors with a deep gratitude.

And I recall that the Christian's hall-marks are humility and self-denying service. That is the sainthood to which we are called. And we shall fulfill our obligations to God and man, the better because we remember the saints who left their stained-glass windows and jumped from their pedestals to meet men in their need.

> For all the saints who from their labors rest,
>
> Who Thee by faith, before the world confessed
>
> Thy name, O Jesus, be for ever blest.

As a concluding story, let me relate a Prayer Meeting in one of the Southern States of America held by colored people.

> *Leader:* O Lord we bless Thee for the glorious company of the Apostles.
>
> *Devout old lady from the back of the Hall:* Glory be to God.
>
> *Leader:* And we bless Thee for the goodly fellowship of the prophets.
>
> *The old lady again:* Glory be to God.
>
> *Leader:* And we bless thee for the goodly fellowship of the martyrs.
>
> *Old lady a third time:* Glory to God.
>
> *Leader in a subdued tome:* But they're all dead . . . O Lord, they're all dead.
>
> *Old lady shouting:* Glory be to God, that's a lie!

Her interjection was greeted by a chorus of "Hallelujahs!"

THE LIVING UNION OF CHRIST AND HIS DISCIPLES

An Expository Sermon

"I am the Vine and ye are the branches."
—John 15:1–10

The Setting

"I AM the vine and ye are the branches." These wonderful words about the living union of the Lord and his disciples were spoken in the closing darkness of our Savior's life, in the last hours before the curtain fell on the finale of the Cross.

We are to picture the Master and his disciples, leaving the Upper Room with minds full of the meaning of the Last Supper and the First Communion. For a time they walk in the silence through the dark street, and enter the Temple Court. And there in front of them, gleaming in the light of the full moon was the great Golden Vine that trailed over the Temple Porch, the symbol of the life of Israel entwined about the sanctuary of God. That symbol on the Temple Porch was as familiar in the history of Israel, as the banner of St. George is in the history of England.

As they look at it in the moonlight, a gentle smile plays upon the lips of the Lord, and he raises his forefinger to the golden vine as he says: "I am the vine, the true vine."

What is his meaning? By implication, in the first place, he reminds the disciples of the false vine, Israel. The true vine stands for what Israel was called by God to be. From the very dawn of Hebrew history there had been a community conscious of a divine mission. Its origin is recorded in the Call of Abraham, in whom all the families of the earth were to be blessed. Centuries pass and the people are still disloyal to God and the great eighth century Prophets despair of the possibility of the whole people making the perfect response to God's righteousness. They claim that only a remnant will fulfill God's purpose, then even this modified hope proves too high. The final intuition of the Old Testament culminates in Isaiah's prophecy of the Suffering Servant, who will be the one and only individual in whom the whole significance of Israel will be centered. He will be the Messiah, offering the perfect response to God. So it came to pass, and Jesus knew at that moment that all the hopes of the years were fulfilled in him. Jesus himself is the true vine. The tree that was planted on Calvary has shoots going out into the entire world. From the days of the Cross and Resurrection onwards, the Chosen People are no longer confined to the sons of Abraham, but it is the society of those who have received the Divine Word spoken in him. From that time onwards, the Chosen People is one man in Christ Jesus. For his life is offered that it may flow in our veins. And as Jesus speaks these solemn words, the disciples know a high and holy exultation in their hearts; for, at last, God's Promises are being fulfilled in Christ, the true Vine.

I Am the Vine, the True Vine

There is second meaning here. Why should Jesus have chosen that as his sign? Why not one of the other necessities that sustained the chosen people: bread or oil? Hamilton King asks this question in her poem: "The Disciples":

> The living Vine, Christ chose it for himself.
> God gave to man for use and sustenance.
> Corn, wine and oils and each of these is good:
> And Christ is bread of life and Light of Life.
> But yet he did not chose the summer corn,
> That shoots up straight and free in one quick growth
> And has its day, is done, and springs no more:
> Nor yet the olive, all whose boughs are spread
> In the soft air and never lose a leaf,
> Flowering and fruitful in perpetual peace;
> But only this for Him and His in one-
> The everlasting, ever quickening Vine,
> That gives the heat and passion of the world
> Through its own life-blood, still renewed and shed.

The Living Union of Christ and His Disciples

The answer is that this, above all nature's plants, typified his cross and Resurrection. It was a botanical sermon. The vine lives to give its life-blood. Its flower is small, but its fruit is abundant; and when that fruit is mature and the vine has for a moment become most glorious, the treasure of the grapes is torn down and the vine is cut back to the stem. The Son of God was made perfect in the things that he suffered. On the Cross was completed his offering to the Father when his life, in its supreme beauty of holiness, was cut off. The rich red juice of the vine was the effectual reminder of the blood that would flow from the crushed body of the Lord on the cross-tree.

But the vine is also the symbol of the Resurrection. It is, as the poem reminds us, "The everlasting, ever quickening vine." Though its fruit is cut off, it puts forth each year bright shoots of living green, perpetually renewing itself. So is Christ. One moment, on the Cross, the plant of his life dies in all its glory of obedience; the next, three days later, there is a blossoming of eternity.

So, on this solemn evening of his betrayal and sacrifice, he reminds his disciples, by the fruit the vine in the Last Supper and by the vine trailing over the Temple Porch that, at last, the promises of God have come true, that the Kingdom of God is to be instantly realized in his Cross and Resurrection.

His Disciples

He goes on. "I am the vine: ye are the branches ... Abide in me and I in you." He speaks of Failure and of Success.

He talks of success first: "He that abideth in me and I in him, he it is that beareth fruit in abundance, because apart from me, ye can do nothing."

Then he speaks of failure: "If a man abide not in me, he is cast forth as a branch and is withered; and they gather them, and cast them into the fire, and they are burned."

O, disciples of Christ, here is a solemn warning. Out of the twelve who had known Christ in the days of his flesh, shared his lonely vigils of prayer on the mountain-tops, and had a part in his glorious successes on the plains below in teaching and healing, one of them was to betray him. Do not presume on your friendship with Christ. Just as the little group of disciples broke out in consternation in the Upper Room, when Jesus foretold that one of them should betray him, just as they looked anxiously to the right and to the left and asked in fear: "Lord, is it I? Lord, is it I?" So should you. Judas thought that he was one of the branches, firmly attached to the Vine. But the branch withered and he came to a miserable end. He had failed Christ, missed the meaning of life. No wonder he snapped the threads of his own life. His soul had already committed suicide. His body was only following suit.

I tell you that whatever the world thinks, the man who departs from Christ, departs from life. He may think that he is flourishing like the bay tree, respected, successful, a well-known figure. But in reality he is only dead wood, making pretence, mere rotten wood. He may boast an obituary notice in *The Times*, but this name is blotted out of the Lamb's Book of Life. His condemnation is written: "Apart from me ye can do nothing." "Live for self; you live in vain/ Live for Christ; you live again."

What, then, is success? It is to abide in Christ, to choose the life of sacrifice instead of security, to follow in the footsteps which have the nail-prints in them, to enter into the sufferings of Christ for his world as yet unredeemed, to lose yourself for his sake that you may find it. This is to make life a success. To this end were you born.

Christ calls to the heroic in us. It is only the superficial, the selfish, and the safe, who are deaf to his challenge and blind to his vision. Men and women, you have sacrificed for patriotism, you have lived dangerously, refused to quit the battlefield, lived on meager rations. Shall you do less for Christ? He wants men and women who will attempt the risks of faith, will brave adventure in witness, risking the taunts and sarcasms of men. He wants men and women who will live on meager rations and contribute sacrificially to his cause.

Do you remember the splendid scene in Shakespeare's *King Henry the Fifth* on the night before the Battle of Agincourt? The weary King goes from tent to tent in the darkness, encouraging his men, enfeebled by sickness, exhausted from marching and utterly unprepared for the battle next day with a superior enemy. Do you recall how he appeals to the heroic in them?

> He which hath no stomach to this fight
>
> Let him depart; his passport shall be made
>
> And crowns for convoy put into his purse:
>
> We would not die in that man's company
>
> That fears his fellowship to die with us.

So does the king excommunicate cowards. Then by his courage, he binds himself to his men.

> We few, we happy few, we band of brothers;
>
> For he today that sheds his blood with me
>
> Shall be my brother; be he ne'er so vile

This day shall gentle his condition:

And gentlemen in England now abed

Shall think themselves accurs'd they were not here

And hold their manhoods cheap whiles any speaks

That fought with us upon St. Crispin's day. (Act IV, iii)

So, Christ warns us that to maintain the Christian faith in days when multitudes have departed from it, will mean struggle. Who has no stomach for this fight, might as well depart.

But, we few, we happy band of brothers, the church militant, are led in the struggle by the brave King of the Cross, whose scarlet and sacred wounds are more splendid than the finest rubies. As he, the true Vine, allowed his body to be crushed on Calvary, as wine is crushed from the grapes, he calls us to be spent, exhausted, to spill our very blood in his service. That and that alone, is success.

Christ the hero calls for heroes today.

SAINTS ALIVE

To all that be in Rome, beloved of God, called to be saints.
—Romans 1:7

If I were to ask you what kind of picture came into your head, when you heard me read this text, and especially the words *called to be saints*, I believe the word irrelevant would sum all the images up.

"Saint" in Rome immediately suggests a man with a halo in a stained-glass window; a legendary story of incredible miracles performed in a credulous age; an M.G.M. picture with a purple-faced emperor in a purple robe calling Roman soldiers to push beautiful blonde starlets into an arena of lions with hungry open maws. The whole impression is antiquarian, spectacular, make-believe, a picture too good to be true. Saints seem to be cardboard heroes, smugly self-satisfied, with a private telephone wire to God. Saints alive, you say, those escapists in their monasteries and nunneries they never even lived, shut up in living tombs. If the price of perfection is to forgo wealth, marriage, position and power in the world, they are welcome to it. *But that's not for me.*

All this only goes to show that we are accepting a stereotype, instead of the rich humanity of the servant-saints. The first mistake is to think they are all alike, they are all conventional. The saints are as varied a group of sanctified human personalities as you could find.

Take two contemporaries. There was Francesco Bernadone. His father was a commercial traveler in silks who was so frequently traveling to France for his exquisite materials fabricated by the silk worms of Lyons, that he called his boy French one, Francesco. That boy was the brightest of bright sparks, always playing tricks on the villagers; serenading the local girls with his guitar on the hot summer evenings; enjoying the company of the inn, as he and his cronies, sang, danced and drank until the small hours. That joyousness he carried over into his conversation; that impulsive generosity and camaraderie impelled him to count even the dreaded leper, and the outcast robber as his friend. That was Francis of Assisi, the gay troubadour of God.

Now for the complete contrast with him. Thomas of Aquino was the quiet, solid, reflective son of an Italian nobleman who sent him to the Monastery of neighboring Monte Cassino in the hope that when he became Abbot he would transfer its wealth to the home treasury. When his brothers heard that he intended to become a Dominican monk, to fight the good fight of capturing men's intellects for Christ and his church, they waylaid him, thrust him into prison for a year, attempted to compromise his otherworldliness by thrusting a beautiful temptress into his cell. He went to Paris to study under the greatest scientist of his day, Albertus Magnus. Someone jestingly referred to this bulky Thomas as vast hulk of an ox. Yes, said Albert, but soon the world will hear his bellowing. And, quite in keeping with his intense application to philosophy, science and the science of God, theology, is the story told of him being entertained by King Louis of France at a State banquet, with the lords, ladies, cardinals, and generals. There was a sudden pause in the laughter, wit, anecdotes and banter and in the unaccustomed silence, Thomas Aquinas's great fist hammered on the table, and he muttered quietly: "Now I have found an argument that will silence the heretics." He carried into his calling the unceasing curiosity and humility of a great thinker. Francis loved people into the acceptance of God; Thomas outthought their prejudices and doubts to win them to God. They were men of different temperaments, of different origins, of different types of services yet marvelously alive today for our encouragements.

Perhaps, someone interjects, what you have said is true of Roman Catholicism; both your examples are taken from that large segment of the Christian church. Is it also true of Protestantism?

Let me give a brief answer to that question by reminding you that Protestantism has also its working servant saints of many races, and of many different denominations and types. Turn to the left-wing of Protestantism, and there you will find John Woolman, the American Quaker abolitionist who felt every shackle on every Negro slave he met as an iron band constricting his own heart and who persuaded the entire religious community of friends to release their slaves, decades before the American Revolution and over a century before the tragic outbreak of the American Civil War. Or, take John Bunyan, the Baptist mender of pots and pans, the Puritan saint and immortal allegorist whose *Pilgrim's Progress* stood beside the Bible as the second essential book in England and New England.

So do I need to remind you that William Temple, the greatest Archbishop of Canterbury since Anselm and Thomas à Beckett was a saint who mated intellectual depth with social compassion and inter-church zeal? Saints alive! That man has not been dead fifteen year, a saint of our own time. Or, take another, Bishop Brent, of the Protestant Episcopal Church, whose entire life was given to the fulfillment of Christ's High Priestly Prayer that all his disciples might be one that the world may believe. Then there was Kagawa, the saint in the slums of Japan, as there is Schweitzer, the theologian, musician, and medical saint on the Ogowe River in French Equatorial Africa, or Simone Weil the philosopher-factory worker, or Elizabeth Fry.

My text will fast become a pretext, if I do not refer you to it. It makes three things clear:

1. The calling of every Christian, not of the elect or the select, is to be a saint.

All, even the most unlikely, are called, summoned by God in Christ to dedicate their gifts, aptitudes and training. God can use your joy, your intellectual curiosity, your unconventional daring, your distinctive traits of personality so that his holy charm, his graciousness can shine through you, his generous reconciling love be channeled through you. The saints are not born, they are made; often they are re-made, that they may be conformed more and more to the image of his Son. Saints are literally those in the process of being sanctified.

2. How can we accept such a thrilling yet daunting calling?

We are called to be saints, beloved God. That is the clue. It is not my faint grip of Christ by faith that counts; it is his firm and unshakable grasp of me that counts. The story is told of Count Nikolas Von Zinzendorff. As an unheeded young man, he visited an art-gallery to pass an idle hour. His eyes were soon transfixed by a vivid representation of the Crucifixion. He saw that sacred head sore wounded with the sarcastic crown of thorns askew upon the noble forehead, the hands nailed in mute appeal, the sword thrusts in Our Lord's side, and the eyes seemed to follow, to follow him, saying: "Is it nothing to all you who pass by?" Without any external gestures, Zinzendorff murmured to himself: "You have done all this for me; what must I do for you?" The call to sainthood that makes the ordinary man extraordinary, the unlikeliest youth the most likeable saint and servant of God, is the sense of God's sheer generosity in Christ. In simplest terms:

> Were the whole realm of nature mine
> That were an offering far too small,
> Love so amazing, so divine,
> Demands my life, my soul, my all.

This assurance impels the saint to go the second mile and nerves him to face all difficulties. "I can do all things through Christ which strengtheneth me." "For neither life, nor death, nor things present, nor things to come; nor height, nor depth, nor any created thing can separate-us from the love of Christ." "Nay in all things we are more than conquerors."

3. Finally, the place of our calling:

It is not in the cloisters, but in the crowd, as C.S. Lewis put it. "To all that are in Rome, called to be saints, beloved of God." It was in the place of their former defeat that the first disciples became apostles of the faith in the crucified and risen Christ. In Jerusalem where they had all forsaken Christ and fled, they were to be Christ's witnesses. Later it was to be in the heart of the greatest Empire then known to the world; in the majestic capital that had succeeded Athens as the cultural center of the world; as the showplace where victorious legionaries returned with the spoils of war defeated kings, commoners and all their treasure; where the majesty of Roman Law was first enacted. Here the statesman, the philosopher, the orator, and the patrician ruled. And Christianity's attempt to gain this citadel must have seemed like the attempt of mosquitoes to subdue a lion. Go to Rome today, as I did many Easters ago, and I warrant that, while you will be impressed by the pageantry and splendor of St. Peter's, you will be far more impressed by the simplicity of the faith of the saints that endured the life of the catacombs.

Where is your Rome? In the heart of this college for the next few years, in your profession, in your home and married life, wherever God has set you, or will set you. It is precisely there, not in any cloistered equivalent, that you are summoned to face the jeers and sneers, the snide and sarcastic remarks, the temptations to be one other faceless member of the anonymous crowd, and to recognize your responsibility to be a worker and servant saint of God. At the beginning, I said that it was wrong to think of saints as remote, stained-glass window types. But if you think of a saint as one through whose personality the light of God shines through, less and less dirtied by the compromises and deceits and shabbiness of half-men, you are near the truth. "Let your light so shine before men that they may glorify your father which is in Heaven." This is the transparent integrity that God desires and mankind needs.

And now unto him who is able to do abundantly above all that we can think or ask, to him, be glory in the church, through Christ Jesus, world without end.

AMEN

I BELIEVE
IN THE FORGIVENESS OF SINS

SIN IS REBELLION AGAINST GOD

My sin is ever before me. Against Thee, Thee only have I sinned. . . .
Behold. I was shapen in iniquity . . . A broken and a contrite heart
Thou wilt not despise.

Psalm 11:3–5 and 17

THESE WORDS will seem to many of us remote and exaggerated and irrelevant, a museum exhibit of ancient fervid religious emotionalism. They seem as remote as old rusty Roman coins, or Victorian penny-farthing, or a fossil. We have never felt like that about our shortcomings. We are not at all sure that we are called upon to feel like that. Tradition tells us that this confession was wrung out of David **through** remorse for a particular brutal act: murder and adultery, no less. That, we would say, accounts for the extravagant tone. And because of that it can have no relation to the confessions of quiet respectable people like ourselves who, thank God, have never known such violent wickedness. Is that all? I want to put it to you that underlying these words of confession are permanent realities and necessities of the moral and spiritual life. We must think of these things, even if we use different language to describe them.

First **my sin is ever before me.** Well, of course, how could it be otherwise, a sin like that? From the moment of its occurrence, David must have been aware of a recurrent and penetrating disquiet pervading his whole being and soaking through every moment and activity of his life. He could not get the thing out of his mind. If he did succeed in driving the thing away, it left behind it an atmosphere of unhappiness, apprehension and degradation, which no effort of will can dispel.

It is like some course, cheap cigar which a man might smoke and throw away but which leaves behind it a heavy stale odor, with which everything in the room now reeks. There was no escaping it. This had been so from the first, but how much more so now that Nathan's words had bidden him go and look at it in all its ugliness. Whatever he does, wherever he goes, he is the man who did that kind of thing. He hears, echoing down every corridor of his mind, Nathan's words "Thou art the man."

He knows in his heart of hearts that no matter what glorious success attends his other enterprises, he remains a despicable failure "My sin is before me."

Now, what conceivable relation has this to you and me? Surely it has. It is absolutely true to say that a man, any man, who does not in his thought of God feel a profound disquietude about himself, is not seeing things as they really are at all. There is something radically wrong, when we confess our sins with no more reverberation of feeling than when we mention our lumbago or sciatica. Surely there is a blatant insincerity and humbug, that having confessed myself **a miserable sinner** in the presence **of God**, I will go forth and allow none of my fellows to criticize me save at the price of my anger and resentment. We will allow no man to play Nathan to us, to say "thou art the man" in this or that and yet we have confessed that we are such men to God.

How many men have not said cruel and wounding things to one another, and when the evil and the hurt of the anger was pointed out to him, has not replied. "Yes, I oughtn't to have said it; but there I am like that: I break out suddenly; my bark is worse than my bite."

And after that the man has justified himself and dismisses the matter from his mind. He has confessed his sin as he might acknowledge the color of his socks or the size of his hat.

What lies behind this attitude? There lies behind it the failure to realize that his supreme concern in life is doing the will of God, goodness. When you begin to grasp that truth, when you see that the first thing in every situation is to walk by the rule of God and not by any other standard; when you have settled it with yourself that every success in life, no matter how brilliant it is, is after all a tinsel and a tawdry thing, if you have not mastered your own soul by surrendering it to the high ends of truth and goodness, then and only then, will you be constrained to cry out and mean it, "My sin is ever present with me." It took a frightful moral collapse to make David thus conscious that nothing mattered, except to be ruled by righteousness in his own soul, and from that point of view he was, despite the outward splendor of his reign, a pitiable failure. Must we, because our unrighteousness takes a politer and more refined form, miss the cleansing revelation that came to him? We, at least, have what David did not have, to strike through our blindness, the light which is in Jesus Christ Our Lord.

(2) "Against Thee, Thee only have I sinned." What is the point of this outburst? He had sinned against Uriah and against Bathsheba, sinned abominably. What is the force of this word "only"? Can we omit it?

Sin Is Rebellion Against God

I do not want to leave it out, because by its very unexpectedness it challenges and taunts our ways of thought, just where they need challenging. It signifies the truth, so typical of biblical religion, that the character of sin is not first and foremost in the relations which it involves us with our fellows, bad as they may be, but in the relationship it involves us in with God. To bring in God is to deepen our thought of sin.

It is to bring home the fact that sin is not a transgression against the law or an offence against others, like traveling without a ticket, or buying in the black-market. It is rebellion against God. Indeed, as the Cross shows us, sin is spitting in the face of God.

I want you to observe what a difference the dimension of God makes in David's confession. Imagine a David, with decent human instincts, but without any deep awareness of God, pondering over what he had done. Listen to his thoughts: "Yes, it was a caddish thing to put Uriah out of the way like that. I ought not to have done it. I have let myself down badly. I must keep a grip on myself in future, live a more disciplined life. The past is deplorable but it's no good worrying over it. What's done can't be undone. Probably Uriah would have fallen in the battle in any case, and death comes to us all sooner or later. It's a good thing anyway that nobody will know that I was behind his death."

So with a few regrets, with facile resolution, calling in tomorrow's discipline to compensate for today's indulgence, he puts the thing behind him. Yes, and it won't be long before he commits the same acts again for he does not feel stained by them, rebuked by the holiness and the majesty of God.

Now listen to the real David. Instantly, in the living presence of God, all such easy thoughts and phrases are scorched and evaporated out of his soul by a burning heat. The thing that has happened is now seen to be far more dreadful. No comfort now in the thought that no one knows, when One so inexorable, so inescapable knows. No comfort now in the thought that what's done cannot be undone: indeed that is the terrifying thought for the future. Uriah dead is Uriah done with, but God you can't be done with. No comfort now in making cheery resolutions for the future, when the whole superstructure of your life has been shaken off its foundation in God. Do you see my meaning? The whole thing is now so tragic, so deep, because God is in it, Uriah, Bathsheba, David, what are they? In a few short years they will all be dead in any case, forgotten, the heat and passion and cruelty and suffering vanished like a vapor. But Uriah, Bathsheba, David **plus God**, that is an infinite equation, "It is against Thee, Thee only, I have sinned."

There is nothing that this overclouded modern world needs more than a recovery of the sense of God in relation to evil. Our first thought is of the self-centered aspect of our actions. We trace out the **social** consequences of sins, we appeal to ourselves to be different because the consequences are so painful. We are encouraged to refrain from lust by warning pictures in railway stations that show a smiling baby whose forehead is shadowed by the dreadful initials V. D. Whereas St. Paul and every great Christian afterwards would have emphasized not the painful consequences but the insult to God, the insult to ourselves made in his image. "Know ye not that ye are a temple of the Holy Ghost?"

No, the religion of the Bible is not based upon calculations of the effect of our actions on man, but on the high and holy standard of achieving God's will. The world will be better, when it realizes how evil it is, and can say: "It is against Thee, Thee only I have sinned."

(3) "Behold in iniquity was I born and in sin did my mother conceive me."

Is it an extravagance? An attempt to shift the blame? A refuge in talk of heredity and environment? No, a deep perception of spiritual truth. David began to see how complex and deep rooted was his sinfulness, how subtly pervasive, how it soaks and seeps through his whole being! Imagine David asking himself how he, of all people with his past history, his lofty aspiration, his calling as monarch of God's people, had fallen so low. He saw that the fall was not a sudden declension from righteousness. All down the years he had indulged himself, that his whole being had for years been punctured with a thousand moral leaks into everything had crept, a corruption of insincerity and self-seeking. It's now plain to him that this had always been his nature. "For behold I was shapen in iniquity and in sin did my mother conceive me, for behold Thou desirest truth in the inward parts!" The inward parts! How can a man cleanse himself? How can the unclean make clean? Therefore he cries again "Make me a clean heart O God, renew a right spirit within me."

"A broken and contrite heart thou wilt not despise." Is that all? Just one thing more. Out of this heart-searching and sense of God's judgment, this contrition and broken-heartedness, there came to the Psalmist a profound sense of God's nearness and forgiveness. He knew that the broken and contrite heart he does not despise, for if he despises, why should he have taken the trouble to break it? The holiness which condemns is the holiness which holds. To see that is at once to be penitent and to be forgiven.

Will you think of these things? If you do, they will lead you right into the presence of the Cross of Christ. In the Cross is given to us the final **revelation** of the righteousness of God, the love which utterly condemns and utterly holds you at the same time. To see that, is to be forgiven, to have a clean heart and a clean start.

I BELIEVE
IN THE LIFE ETERNAL

IMMORTALITY

Our Savior Jesus Christ who abolished death, and brought life and immortality to light through the Gospels.

—II Timothy 1:10

I would remind you that this reassuring and radiant creed was penned by a political prisoner in a condemned cell. He is writing in the dim light to a discouraged young minister.

"No shrinking," he says to Timothy "for God has given us a spirit not of timorousness, but of power and love and discipline." Then he drives home his point. "Timothy you mustn't be ashamed to witness to your Lord; you mustn't be ashamed of my being in prison; remember Our Savior Jesus Christ, who abolished death and brought life and immortality to light through the Gospel."

Timothy and every young Christian after him who has to face the perils for Christ's sake are meant to understand that the Resurrection of Jesus Christ is the liquidation of death. Yes, and to understand that Jesus Christ brings life as well as eternal life, and to be able to shout with St. Paul: "O death, where is thy sting, O grave where is thy victory? Thanks be to God who giveth us the victory through our Lord Jesus Christ."

I. What Is This Gift of Immortal Life?

This gift of immortal life, that was the source of Paul's faith, means liberation. That is a word that has taken new meaning, for every friend who addresses a letter to our fighting men with the great initials B.L.A.—that is, British Liberation Army—beneath it, realizes its full meaning.

Perhaps it is a word that the relatives of prisoners-of-war can best understand. Liberation for them means the home-coming of their loved ones after five years or more of silence only lightened by the arrival of postcards and brief, all too brief, letters. All that waiting is ended and they are delirious with joy. The day of liberation is at hand!

Perhaps also this is a word that the downtrodden people of Holland and Denmark and Belgium and the best of Germans understand, though they must be stunned and dazed today. But they will be giving our men a welcome, if it is only to share what little there is in some of the meager larders of the dispossessed.

But liberation means more than this in St. Paul's words and in the glorious Gospel. It is the eternal home-coming! What are twenty, thirty, forty, fifty, sixty, seventy, eighty years compared with eternity! What is liberation from the evil clutches of the Gestapo, compared with liberation from death, the last enemy that shall be destroyed in our passing hence! Death is abolished, liquidated, annihilated by the Resurrection of Jesus Christ! Whatever happens now . . . and I am not being casual, for the suffering of this life are poignantly and passionately real; but whatever happens now, Christ's Resurrection means a home-coming for ever!"In my Father's house are many mansions." And Christ is there waiting in his own good time to welcome every travel-stained pilgrim to the twinkling lights of home.

> We travel the dusty road till the light of day grows dim
> The sunset shows us spires away on the world's rim.

Surely we can see what a liberation this is! Here we are, pretty creatures of a few days, and suddenly it comes home that we are made for eternity, that we shall live as long as God himself. Our beloved died: and so we laid them to rest and that was all. We left the grave-side with resignation or with a smile that hurt more than tears. "No!" say the Scriptures, they are not dead, they are alive, more richly and full than before in that wonderful world where there are no more pains and failing powers; but where they are, all young and well and strong again, and serve him day and night and never need to rest at all. Surely, this is liberation from fear, from anxiety, and from despair. "Blessed be God who hath brought life and immortality to light through the Gospel." Blessed be Christ, the pioneer from the grave, the first to cross the frontier and to return.

II. This Gospel of Eternal Life We Do Well to Remember; It Is Also the Doom of Evil

Here again we can find an analogy in the situation across the Channel. As surely as the combined onslaught of the American, Russian and British armies means death to the vile Nazi movement that pitted itself against God and persecuted his church; as surely as the Gestapo shall find that justice is

Immortality

stronger than truncheons or triggers, so the Resurrection of Jesus Christ is the first installment of God's victory over evil.

So Peter proclaimed "This Jesus whom ye crucified, Him hath God raised from the dead and made Him to be Lord." God has made this world so that if men break laws of God, they shatter themselves. Sometimes that judgment comes in History, as it comes today with a rising crescendo of fury, terrible as an army with banners. Sometimes that judgment waits until the Judgment Day of Christ. Sometimes that judgment of God comes in personal life, where the soul has so neglected the spiritual help of Christ and his church, that it is an empty vault, a mask of a face covering sheer emptiness. Then God takes from it one by one the earthly treasures that it valued, until it is brought back to see the poor, perishing thing that it has become.

But however it comes, wherever it comes, the Resurrection proves that the Lord God omnipotent reigneth, that evil is suicide: Literally murdering one's own future life, and maiming one's present life.

We sometimes talk foolishly about the future of Christianity. We let ourselves wonder what the ultimate issue between goodness and evil will be. Is it possible that the forces of evil will overwhelm the forces of Christ and that these powers will be too strong for him? Let the thought die on your lips. For anyone who reads his life knows that this is impossible. "He showed himself alive after his passion." "He has the keys of heaven and Hades." "Evil is done for." "The Lord omnipotent reigneth." That is the song of the redeemed in heaven.

There is an earthly battle to fight, but the issue is certain. You do right to concern yourself with the skirmishes of today, the fight for social justice, the struggle for world justice ... You must not let the demonic forces of evil, the insolence and vileness of some who flaunt their sins, shake your faith. Evil is doomed. God has vindicated his beloved Son's right to rule as King over the souls of men. "Here on this Rock" said Jesus once, "I will build my church." The tides of unbelief shall never shake it!

Four hundred years ago, when Francis Xavier set out on the Christian mission in the East, he said a magnificent thing. "You may be absolutely certain about one thing," he declared, "**the devil will be tremendously sorry to see the company of the Name of Jesus enter China.**" Then he added "Just imagine! A thing as vile as I am to bring down such a vast reputation as the devil's! What great glory to God!"

Eternal life is the promise that through the Resurrection of Jesus Christ, goodness is triumphant in the world's battle between the children of light and the children of darkness. That is joy for the struggler.

Eternal life is the promise that for Christ's folk death is a mighty liberation from the prison of life. That is joy for the anxious and bereaved.

Eternal life is the promise that gives comfort to the aged, that the sunsets shall all be followed by sunrises. It was told by Canon Liddon, whom a number of you may have heard when he preached in St. Paul's:

An old Indian officer was recounting his battles of the Indian mutiny and of the striking events in his career. As he described the skirmishes, the battles, the sieges and the hairbreadth escapes, his audience hung breathless in sympathy and excitement. At last, he paused; and to their impressions of wonderment he replied: "I expect to see something much more wonderful than that." As he was over seventy and retired from the army, his listeners looked up into his face with surprise. Again there was a pause and he said in solemn undertone: "I mean . . . the first five minutes after death."

St. John, the seer of Patmos, looked out on the world at the age of ninety, like an eager youth, ready for the Great Adventure and he said: "Beloved now are we the sons of God, and **it doeth not yet appear what we shall be.**" The wonder and the joy and the surprise of it are hidden from us now. But like St. John, we are able to stand on the rim of the world and look out over the wall.

This Gospel of Eternal Life is for all of us, the bereaved, the despondent, the young, the old, the maimed, the sick, the widow and the widower. Pointing to each in turn from the first-born to the dead, the Risen Lord says to his own: "Women, or men, cease your sobbing. I am the Resurrection and the life and whoever believes in Me shall never die. In my Father's house there are many mansions, waiting for every wounded soldier who returns from my war, waiting for you."

And in that day of reunion, we shall be ashamed of doubts and fears, and falling on our knees, we shall exclaim "O Lord Jesus, King and Redeemer, your promises are greater than our dreams!"

ETERNAL LIFE: HERE & HEREAFTER

Sermon Notes

But the gift of God is eternal life through Jesus Christ.

—Romans 6:23

This is life eternal to know Thee, the only true God and Jesus Christ whom Thou didst send.

—John 17:3

If any man is in Christ, he is a new creation.

—II Corinthians 5:17

NOTES: ETERNAL life: two criticisms.

(1) **Puritanism**

"One life at a time, brother, one life at a time."

Art, music, science, history ... are "toys"

William. Lyon Phelps. "The Puritans felt that life was serious but they had faith in the ultimate rightness of things; they believed that this was God's world and that its darkness would be followed by eternal sunshine. . . . The Puritans believed that out of a dark soil bright showers would spring; the modern pessimist offers us no flowers, but more dirt."

(2) Second criticism: **Quietism**

The social reformer is a dupe: chloroform.

The psychologist; compensatory mechanism.

Aldous Huxley: "Jesting Pilate." Admirers of India are unanimous in praising Hindu spirituality. I cannot agree with them. To my mind, spirituality is the primal curse of India and the cause of her misfortunes. It is this preoccupation with spiritual realities, different from the actual historical realities of common life that has kept millions upon millions of men and women content, through centuries with a lot unworthy of human beings. A little less spirituality and the Indians would now be free from foreign dominion and from the tyranny of their own prejudices and traditions. There would be less dirt and more food. There would be fewer Maharajas with Rolls Royces and more schools.

What is the answer to these criticisms?

It is a misunderstanding: the Christian knows that eternal life is not survival; it is transformation here and now. It is a new dimension and a new depth in life. It is fellowship with God now: "This is life eternal to know Thee the only true God and Him whom thou didst send, even Jesus Christ."

(3) I John 3:14: Eternal life is a present possession. "We know that we have crossed over from death to life because we love the brethren."

Dr. F. W. Robertson of Brighton declared this message with power on Easter day, in 1853. He said "There are men in whom the Resurrection already begun makes the Resurrection credible. In them the spirit of the Risen Christ works already; and they have mounted with him from the grave. Their step is as free as if the clay of the sepulcher had been shaken off, and their heart, are lighter than those of other men; and there is in them an unearthly triumph which they are unable to express. They have risen above the narrowness of life, and all that is petty, ungenerous and mean. They have risen above fear: they have risen above self."

He ends: "he believes in a Resurrection because the Resurrection has begun in himself."

"What shall I do to inherit eternal life?"

"Yet one thing thou teachest. Sell all your goods and feed the poor."

TERMINUS BECOMES TUNNEL

I Believe in the Resurrection of the Body and the Life Everlasting

> *He showed himself alive after His Passion.*
> —Acts 1:3

THAT IS the most staggering sentence in the New Testament. The universe has happened; the unpredictable has occurred. The impenetrable curtain dividing the end of this life from the inscrutable mystery beyond has been drawn back for an instant. Christ's crimson sunset on Calvary followed by the midnight of human hopes, has been succeeded by a resplendent dawn. A full-stop had become a comma; a terminus becomes a tunnel; in the very centre of the black wall of death there opens the golden-gate and out of it walks the Prince of life. Words cannot describe the novelty, the joy, the triumph of the disciples as they announced that showed himself alive after his passion! Henceforth man's greatest enemy death had lost much of its power.

Have you ever looked closely at the pictures of the great Protestant artist Rembrandt? If you have, you will have noticed that the shadows are not merely dark or cold grey; they are luminous. They gleam with a faint golden light; they glisten with the promise of further brightness. There is no such thing as unrelieved gloom in a Rembrandt picture. There is now no such thing as unrelieved gloom in a Christian's life.

We must try and live in the atmosphere of excitement which fills this glowing statement we take as our text. The disciples were welcoming a pioneer back from the most tremendous adventure, one who had returned from the frontiers of the other world.

The disciples must have felt as excited as we did watching the aerial combats of the Battle of Britain. These brave pilots of ours had the fascination of men venturing on the brink of death. One bullet on the edge of the barrier of the unseen and they would have toppled over into eternity. What riveted the attention was not only that they were contending in the clouds and in the wide spaces of sea and land, but the fact that they were hovering on the boundary of life, between this world and the next. Their far-flung struggle was a crisis on the frontier of human-existence.

The disciples knew that the crucifixion of Christ was such a crisis, but they had made up their minds that the battle was lost. Then, surprisingly, Christ returned triumphantly on to the scene. He had penetrated the secret of that hidden country beyond Jordan; he was the first to receive a passport to earth from the New Jerusalem. This was history. It was absolutely unique: Christ was the first and only explorer of that country that lies beyond the stars! And all the vague dreams and pious hopes of good people through the centuries were translated in his return to reality. The Resurrection was no longer a dream, a fantasy, a possibility. It was actuality, certainty. Now it was this fact that the disciples declared was proof positive that God had declared Jesus to be the Christ, the King of Kings. The same fact transformed the disciples from cowards to crusaders. The same fact produced the Christian Sunday and the early morning Communion service. The same made possible the martyrdom of Stephen and the others, for whom death was a leap not into darkness but into the arms of Christ.

Take the Resurrection out of Christianity and the whole edifice drops to the ground; take the Resurrection out of human life and you make all our ideals a hollow, resounding mockery. You break the sword of justice in two; you condemn our existence to the doom of butterflies and bees and beetles. No one has put it more starkly and succinctly than St. Paul. "If in this life only we have hope in Christ, we are of all men most pitiable."

If I doubted that the Resurrection were true, I should resign from this church. For it is the countersign of God that gives the authority to the teaching of Christ, that converts it from mere guesswork into Divine truth. The ultimate meaning of the Christian faith and human life stand or fall by the Resurrection.

The important question is this: What does the Resurrection mean for our Christian life here and now?

I. The Resurrection Means the Doom of Sin

It proclaims nothing less than the final, irrevocable defeat of evil in every shape and form.

Take the book of Revelation, written in the day of battle. There you have a background of smoke and blood and martyrdom and cynical laughter. The home of the Caesars and the church of Christ are locked in a death-grapple. The mailed fists of Nero and Domitian are smashing their way through the dreams of the saints. Here you have the second Babylon, mother of all the abominations of the earth, drunk with the blood of the friends of Jesus, laughing in the intoxication of her triumph, shrieking with fiendish laughter to see the poor pathetic body of Christ being crushed and mangled and battered out of existence. That is what the author of Revelation sees over his shoulder as he writes. What will he say? Will he write "The battle is lost. Our cause is ruined. There is only one thing to do, which is to sue for mercy." Does he write this? No. He writes "Hallelujah! Baylon is fallen, is fallen." And why? At the back of the visible world, behind all his pomp and pride and power, he had seen something which Caesar had never seen, something that spelt the doom of Caesar and of all tyranny; he saw a throne up reared above the earth and, sitting on the right hand of the throne of God, the risen and reigning Christ.

Today sometimes men hold their hands on their hearts and wonder if there is any future for Christianity. Is it possible that force and injustice may prevail? Is it possible that the Jesus whom we love may go down at last before powers that are too strong for him? Those who see the point of the Resurrection know that evil is already done for.

Some may say unbelievingly: "It doesn't look a bit like it. Look at the international scene. Look at our current literature. Look at the chaos of our morals. See how evil flaunts itself in the open. See how it strikes its roots deeper and deeper. I know this; but I also know of a greater power, the power of Christ and his Resurrection.

François Xavier, four hundred years ago, said a magnificent thing about the Christian Mission to the Far-East. "You may be sure of one thing" he declared "the devil will be tremendously sorry to see the Company of the name of Jesus enter China. Just imagine! A thing so vile as I am to bring down such a vast reputation as the devil's. What great glory to God!"

The very mainspring of the Christian's courage is the faith of the Resurrection, that he is not fighting a losing battle.

Fight on then, you who have lost heart. The battle is not the enemy's, it is yours. For the Christ of God did not go down before the powers of evil. He was raised from the dead and sitteth at the right hand of God. He makes his victory yours.

II. The Resurrection Also Means the Comfort of Sorrow

There was a terrible night out on the Galilean lake, when the sudden whirlwind blew; the sea was writhing in fury under the lashes of the storm; the boat struggled in the deep troughs of the waves; the disciples were telling themselves: "Our last hour has come; this is the end." And there was Jesus sleeping through it all. "Master, Master, carest thou not that that we perish?" But that night by the grace of God, they learned this lesson. There is something higher in human experience than life's waves and storms; there is a Christ who rules the waves.

Chesterton has preached this victory of the Cross in a marvelous poem.

> Though giant rains put out the sun,
>
> Here stand I for a sign
>
> Though earth be filled with waters dark
>
> My cup is filled with wine.
>
> Tell to the trembling priests that here
>
> Under the deluge rod,
>
> One nameless, tattered, broken man
>
> Stood up and drank to God.

And God accepted the sacrifice, and turned the gallant tragedy into a glorious victory.

The greatest test of a man's faith is how he faces up to death. If he quails or shivers then, the bravado of his life is seen to be superficial. If he endures at that point, then he stands upon solid convictions.

There was an old Welsh saint, of a former generation, a great soldier of Christ. Christmas Evans they called him. And when the day came for him to die, he bade his friends at his bedside farewell, and turned his face to the wall; and in a little while suddenly they saw him wave his hand triumphantly. "Drive on! Drive on!" he cried as if he could see Christ's chariots coming to him.

If Christ be risen from the dead, then life and death are shorn of their terrors for you. Like the priests of Alsace, recite your *Magnificat* through the crash of bursting shells. Your life is safe; it is hid with Christ in God.

"Tell me" said one of Luther's enemies to him sneeringly, "tell me. When the whole world turns against you, Church, State, princes, people, where will you be then?" "Where shall I be then?" cried the great soul, "Why, then as now, in the hands of Almighty God."

And if Christ be risen from the dead, our spirits ought to be dauntless, too.

Let troubles rise and terrors frown,

And days of darkness fall;

Through Him all dangers we'll defy,

And more than conquer all.

Remember a simple fact: there are no Christian casualties in the good fight. God is keeping watch in the shadows, guarding his own.

Whatever news may come from the battlefront, there is one thing that Christian soldiers may say with complete confidence. In the words of Savanarola: "They may kill me if they please: but they will never, never, never tear the living Christ from my heart."

THE FRUIT
OF BELIEF: JOY

ESSENTIALS OF HAPPINESS

*"These things have I spoken unto you that my joy
might remain in you and that your joy might be full."*
—John 15:11

My theme today is the four essentials of Christian joy.

Why did Jesus Christ come to earth? Many different answers, all of them true, might be given. He came to demonstrate the love of God in His own person. "God so loved that He sent . . ." He came to show the holy hatred God has against sin; for the Cross shows us man spitting in the face of God, insulting Him and His love. "This is the judgment that men preferred darkness rather than light." He came to show that the way of sacrifice is the way to life eternal. "He that loses his life for my sake and the Gospel's shall save it. If a man would follow me, let him take up his gibbet and follow me." And yet, there was another meaning in His divine descent to earth. He came to show us the secret of the art of living, the sources of joy. "I am come that they might have life and have it more abundantly."

"These things have I spoken unto you that joy might remain in you and that your joy might be full." I want you to look with me into the secret sources of joy. We need that desperately these days. We understood something of the horror of sin before, but we have surely learned by now the bewildering grace and love of God in the Bethlehem's cradle, in the shadowed Garden of Gethsemane, in the Cross, and in the thrill of the empty tomb; we know the meaning of sacrifice, and ever more deeply we have come to realize the discipline and hardships of the Christian life. But this word "joy" we need to hear. It speaks to our condition in these days, to all overstrained folks whose nerves are frayed, whose tempers easily roused, and who are uncertain about the future. This is what we need: His joy.

What are the ingredients of Christian joy?

The Fruit of Belief: Joy

(1). First we need a good conscience. I want you to look at a famous dramatic character and to ask yourselves what she needed. That will give you the first ingredient of joy.

The scene is an ante-chamber in the castle of Dunsinane. In one corner a physician and a lady in waiting hold a whispered conversation. Suddenly on the balcony above a candle appears and then a figure of a woman in white, sleep-walking. Her eyes are open, staring and glassy. And she is wringing her hands endlessly as if she would wash them of some fearful stain. They overhear her words and sighs "Here's the smell of the blood still: all the perfumes of Arabia will not sweeten this little hand." And there escapes a three-fold piteous sigh from her lips. The lady-in-waiting says "I would not have such a heart in my bosom for the dignity of the whole body." The doctor says: "This disease is beyond my practice. More needs she the divine than the physician. God, God forgive us all."

This classic scene is the account of a guilty conscience that forbids sleep that troubles the mind that forfeits joy.

So, the first ingredient of happiness is a clear conscience. A man who lives for Christ and by the power of Christ can face his friends and foes alike with a quiet mind. Happy is He who can say: "Thank God I have done my duty." There are no stains on his hands. The righteous man can say of himself: "Who shall ascend unto the hill of the Lord, and who shall enter His holy place? He that hath clean hands and a pure heart."

And, for all of us, tormented and tortured by our failures, we can say with Lady Macbeth's doctor: "God, God forgive us all." And by the crimson stains of the Cross of the Son of God, though our sins be as scarlet, they shall be whiter than snow. We are forgiven. We have a clean start, a new beginning. God will forgive and forget, and give us a quiet mind: "Father, forgive them for they know not what they do." "I have spoken these things that my joy might remain with you . . ." A good conscience is the first secret of Christian joy.

(2). The second ingredient is a soul, free from resentment against others or against life.

The surest way to dispel joy is to nurse bitterness, to feed fat your grudges, to dwell on your disappointments and exaggerate difficulties. The antidote to that is "Whatsoever things are true, whatsoever things are honorable, whatsoever things are pure, whatsoever things are lovely, whatsoever things are of good report, if there be any virtue, and if there be any praise, think on these things." (Phil. 4:8.).

Count your blessings; it is not old-fashioned advice; it is up-to-date as the six o'clock news. My advice to anyone nursing bitterness is to take a large plain white sheet of paper and pencil and catalogue your gratitude. And I should write in capitals on the head of that sheet of paper: Christ died for me and rose again. That is as true for you on the day when you die as it is on the day when you were born. By His death he has given you life, a purpose in life and by His Resurrection; He has given you endless life.

Then I should list every friend that God has given you, and every hour of happiness known in their company.

Then I should catalogue every opportunity God has given me to help others, and every opportunity others have taken to show me kindnesses. I guarantee that if you search your memory honestly and carefully, you will not have paper enough to record your gratitude. I guarantee, too, that you will realize as never before how amazingly good God has been to you. And I am sure, if you make Thanksgiving and Praise the first part of your prayers, there will be fewer requests and petitions in your prayers. Why? You will hardly dare to ask God for more, since He has already given so much. And that will be the beginning of the end of bitterness, complaints, and sorrow.

The secret of Christian joy is increasing gratitude. As that joyous Christian Chesterton once said. "Instead of saying like the old religious poet 'What is man that Thou art mindful of him?' we say like the discontented cabman, "What's this?" or, like the bad-tempered Major in the club: 'Is this a cup fit for a gentleman?' The only way to enjoy even a weed is to feel unworthy of it. The aim of life is appreciation."

"These things have I spoken to you that my joy might remain in you and that your joy might be full."

(3). The third ingredient of happiness is faith: trust. To say, with our blessed Lord: "Father into Thy hands I commend my spirit." That is the way to drive out fear that gnaws at the soul and doubt that brings damp clamminess to cloud the soul.

"An atheist" says John Buchari "is a man who has no invisible means of support." A Christian endures as seeing Him who is invisible.

I like the story of the old American Bishop Quayle; his very name sounds as if he had a tendency to fear. One night when William Quayle was awake, his mind endlessly revolving round and round the difficulties; you know the experience only too well. He heard God speaking to Him: "Quayle, you go to bed; I'll sit up the rest of the night." It was whimsically expressed, but the experience was sound and real. Handle the day's work as well as you can but remember that larger shoulders than yours and a wiser mind than yours are controlling the universe. And you can say "All is well. God is with me. Goodnight."

The Fruit of Belief: Joy

(4). The deepest source of joy is a selfless spirit that forgets itself and its worries in seeking the good of others. We see that sublimely and supremely in our Lord "Who for the joy that was set before Him endured the Cross, despising the shame and is set down at the right hand of God." Seeking the redemption of the world, his own deep and poignant agonies and disappointments, were secondary and unimportant. He said: "Lo, I come to do Thy will!" and he buried self in the service of God and of the world. So and only so, could he endure the Cross, and despise the shame. And only so can we, when our lives are no longer ours but His, when we are hid with Christ in God.

I close with an example of two people who had found this secret in a time of crisis, and there are countless others like them in every church. A Press photographer, recording at great risk the fire-raids on the city of London has said that he missed the picture of a life-time. It was when he saw two elderly nuns walking calmly among the blazing ruins. Around them charred timbers were falling, emitting a cascade of sparks. They were carrying trays of tea to exhausted fire-fighters, unaware of their own danger, heroic, undisturbed. Quiet strength, unmoved radiance, shone from their faces. They had all four secrets of Christian joy. They had:

(1). a clear conscience if God were to call them away at that instant, they were ready.

(2). a life spent in the service of Christ's needy children, which had removed all personal bitterness.

(3). recited a thousand times the words: "I believe in the Resurrection and in the life everlasting." Death had no terrors for them; they trusted.

(4). treasured the crucifix on their breast. It was no mere ornament. It was the symbol of their dedication to Him who endured the cross.

My friends, the ever-living Christ promises you in His service, a clear conscience, the removal of all bitterness, the faith and love that cast out fear and the selflessness of the Cross. All these things as to each soul, as to every listener, He says: "These things have I spoken to you that my joy might remain in you and that your joy might be full; my peace I give unto you."

www.ingramcontent.com/pod-product-compliance
Lightning Source LLC
Chambersburg PA
CBHW071450150426
43191CB00008B/1293